POCKET

INVESTOR

POCKET
INVESTOR

PHILIP RYLAND

THE ECONOMIST IN ASSOCIATION WITH
PROFILE BOOKS LTD

Profile Books Ltd
58A Hatton Garden, London EC1N 8LX

This third edition published by Profile Books Ltd
in association with
The Economist Newspaper Ltd 2000

Typest in Garamond by MacGuru
info@macguru.org.uk

Printed in Italy by
LEGO S.p.a. – Vicenza – Italy

A CIP catalogue record for this book is available
from the British Library

ISBN 1 86197 255 5

CONTENTS

INTRODUCTION

Pocket Investor is one of a series of management titles that is designed to bring clarity to specialist subjects. It is written by Philip Ryland, associate editor of the *Investors Chronicle*, and is divided into three parts.

Part 1 comprises essays on aspects of investment, including the returns to be gained (or not) from investing, the difficulties of beating the stockmarkets, the basics of building an investment portfolio and the techniques used by some of the master investors.

Part 2 is an A–Z of terms used in investment. In this section words in small capitals usually indicate a separate entry. However, all acronyms and abbreviations such as EU and TV are in small capitals even if they have no separate entry.

Part 3 consists of appendices, which provide information on stockmarket returns and performances, investment formulas, a list of accounting terms with their American equivalents and recommended reading.

Other titles in the series are:

Pocket Accounting
Pocket Advertising
Pocket Director
Pocket Economist
Pocket Finance
Pocket International Business Terms
Pocket Internet
Pocket Law
Pocket Manager
Pocket Marketing
Pocket MBA
Pocket Money
Pocket Negotiator
Pocket Strategy

UNDERSTANDING THE BASICS

Those for whom investment is a hidden world might like to tiptoe gently into it by first reading the essays "The returns you can expect from the markets" and "Are excess returns there for the taking?". After that, the following definitions provide the foundations for understanding many aspects of investment.

ARBITRAGE
BALANCE SHEET
BETA
BLACK-SCHOLES OPTION PRICING MODEL
BOND
CAPITAL ASSET PRICING MODEL
CASHFLOW
CLOSED-END FUND
CONVERTIBLE
DERIVATIVES
DISCOUNT RATE
DIVIDEND DISCOUNT MODEL
DIVIDEND YIELD
EARNINGS
EFFICIENT MARKET HYPOTHESIS
EQUITY
FUTURES
GEOMETRIC MEAN
INTERNAL RATE OF RETURN
LEVERAGE
MUTUAL FUND
OPTION
ORDINARY SHARE
PORTFOLIO THEORY
PRICE/EARNINGS RATIO
PROFIT AND LOSS ACCOUNT
RETURN ON CAPITAL
RISK-FREE RATE OF RETURN
STANDARD DEVIATION
TECHNICAL ANALYSIS
TIME VALUE
WARRANT
YIELD TO MATURITY

Part 1

ESSAYS

THE RETURNS YOU CAN EXPECT FROM THE MARKETS

To say that recent years have been wonderful for investors is an understatement. Anyone who had the foresight or good luck 25 years ago to put a lump of capital into a group of shares which turned out to be a good substitute for the s&p 500 index, the most widely quoted benchmark for US stock values, would have seen the value of their investment multiply over 20 times; and that is before taking account of the dividends they would have consistently received. The last ten years have been even better. US common stocks on average rose 4.2 times in the period 1989–99.

The returns generated by US stocks are not exceptional. Look around the world and the picture is similar. Share values in the UK rose 36-fold in the 25 years to the end of 1999 (although the starting base was especially low because the UK was recovering from a particularly nasty bear market in 1974). Even in Japan, where share values ended 1999 still languishing over 50% below the peak they reached in 1989, they were still five times higher than they had been at the end of 1974.

In the dynamic economies of the Pacific Rim the results, not surprisingly, are far more dramatic. At the end of 1999 the Hong Kong stockmarket stood 111 times higher than it had at the end of 1974 and almost seven times above its end-1989 level.

An important consequence of these consistently outstanding returns is that a whole generation of investors – both professional and private – has grown up not knowing the debilitating effects of a savage bear market. The sort of bear market that gripped Wall Street between 1937 and 1941, when the market fell four years out of five, losing 38% of its value in the process. Or that of the UK in 1973 and 1974, when shares fell 31% and 55% respectively. Or the grandfather of them all, the Wall Street Crash, when shares fell persistently for three years so that when the market bottomed out in July 1932 it was 87% below the euphoric peak it reached in September 1929.

In these circumstances, it is tempting to conclude that those with no memories of bitter stockmarkets will be condemned to experience them. The confidence that continues to propel stockmarkets to further highs more or less ensures this; and there is a subclass of Cassandras in the investment world almost urging the optimists on. It is worth asking, however, if it really would be so bad to relive the experiences of the stockmarket's past.

There are data going back 100 years from which to form an opinion. Charles Dow devised his first stockmarket index in 1884 and his Dow Jones Industrial Average dates back to 1897 when it consisted of 12 stocks. It was not until 1915 that the list was increased to 20 stocks and the Dow became a better indicator of the health of United States Inc. A sweeping view of the post-1915 data tells us that reliving history may be quite tolerable.

Splitting returns from the Dow into eight consecutive ten-year periods (see Appendix 1), which brings us up to the end of 1995, reveals two notable things.

- The ten years 1986–95 were the best of the lot by a wide margin. The 12.7% compound growth that the Dow achieved in this period cannot be bettered by any preceding ten-year period. In addition, this superior growth was achieved without the convulsions that so often characterise stockmarkets. This is based on the fact that the standard deviation of stockmarket returns (a common measure of the volatility of stock prices) was lower in 1986–95 than in any other ten-year period.
- Even if the most recent ten years led the field, most of the others were pretty good. In only two periods, 1926–35 and 1966–75, did the Dow finish lower than it started.

It is true that these results are affected by the arbitrary nature of the start date and the choice of ten-year periods. But whichever way the cake was cut, the conclusion would be that although recent returns have been outstanding, investment in the stockmarket for any decently long period, say five years or more, would be highly likely to produce acceptable returns. This conclusion is not threatened if we compare stock returns with those on bonds – as we must because the choice of investments necessarily depends on what is available elsewhere – and then adjust for the eroding effects of inflation.

Using a different set of data, which compares US stock returns with those from best-quality commercial bonds in each of the 11 decades 1891–1999, three significant observations can be made.

- In only one decade out of the 11, the 1930s, have the inflation-adjusted returns from bonds been better than the real returns from equities.
- In just two of the 11 decades have common stocks failed to make a return that was higher than inflation: the period 1910–19 and the 1970s.
- In five of the 11 periods bonds failed to return more than inflation: 1910–19 and the four successive decades from the 1940s to the 1970s.

Nor is the US experience unusual. A similar study for the UK from 1919 onwards by BZW, a leading investment bank, shows that equities have consistently outperformed both gilt-edged stocks and Treasury bills after adjusting for inflation.

Tempting conclusions
It is tempting to reach two conclusions from all this. First, that future investment returns from equities, for example those to be generated over the next 20 years, will not be nearly as good as those achieved in the last 20 years. Future equity

returns may well regress to the long-run average which, incidentally, for the United States in the 80 years 1916–95 is a compound rate of 7.2% per year nominal. Second, that, for the most part, equities will continue to be a better investment than bonds. A third conclusion also presents itself: not only will future equity returns be lower, they will also materialise in a more volatile form. To the extent that any average has its normal proportion of extremes, this is a necessary concomitant of the first conclusion.

Arguably just as remarkable as the rate at which stock values have grown in the last 25 years is the consistency with which returns have arrived. In the 26 years since the last deep bear market in 1973–74, US stocks have finished lower year-on-year just four times. In the UK there have been only three down years in that time and London's All-Share index had a run of 13 years from 1976 finishing the year higher than it started.

Yet in the 84-year history of fully authenticated US stock returns, the Dow Jones Industrial Average has had 27 down years. In the UK the ratio is similar: 28 down years out of 81. In other words, in both markets the loss-making years crop up at the rate of about one in three. The question is, then, in the last two decades what has happened to the losing years? The answer may be that the averages are just waiting to reassert themselves.

Increased volatility in stock returns will matter a little or a lot depending largely on each investor's intended investment horizon. The longer the intended investment period, the less that volatility need be a concern. For evidence of this, consider returns generated in the UK over the 20 years starting in 1974. Imagine that two investors each bought a batch of UK shares during 1974, the year when the UK market plunged because of fears of the twin effects of high oil prices and an old-style socialist government being in power. Assume, also, that one investor was unfortunate enough to have bought shares when the market was at its 1974 peak (that is, before it crashed) and that the other was lucky enough to have bought at the market's low for the year.

After one year the investment performance of the two would be vastly different. Using the returns produced by the All-Share index as a proxy for their returns, the table shows that the unlucky investor would, at worst, have been carrying a 59% capital loss (that is, measuring from the peak at which he bought shares to the trough for the following year). Meanwhile, the lucky investor would, at best, have been running a 159% profit.

Holding period (years)	Returns (% per year)	
	Minimum	Maximum
1	−59	159
5	8	36
10	12	25
15	13	22
20	12	18

However, as the investment horizon lengthens two interesting things happen. First, the unlucky investor moves into profit and his profit stabilises. Whether his investment period is 10, 15 or 20 years the annual return remains about 12%. (Note that profit is being expressed as the annual compound return from the level at which he bought to the market's low point for each year in question.) Second, the gap between the best possible and worst possible investment returns narrows and stabilises. From a gap of 218 percentage points after one year, it regresses to around 13 points after ten years and continues to narrow slowly. Not that the gap is inconsequential. The power of compounding means that for the 20-year holding period an 18% per annum return generates three times as much as a 12% return. For example, $1,000 invested at 18% becomes $27,393, but at 12% it becomes just $9,646.

It is important to realise that 1974 was deliberately chosen as a freakish start date, but freakishly bad from the point of view of what we are trying to prove, which is that satisfactory investment returns are available for all equity investors who are prepared to bide their time.

As further evidence that even at worst the returns from UK equities in 1974–94 were satisfactory, bear in mind that they are shown without the beneficial effects on returns of the dividends paid by ordinary shares. Similarly, these returns are substantially better than those produced by UK government bonds. For example, using slightly different data BZW, an investment bank, has shown that the average rate of return on gilts for 1974–94 after adjusting for inflation, but assuming that dividends bore no tax and were reinvested, was 5.7% a year. In contrast, the corresponding figure for equities was 13.5%.

Risk and reward
One conclusion leaps out from this discussion. It is that, just as capital market theory says, investors are indeed rewarded for taking extra risks. The risks are that over a short period, usually two or three years and rarely more than five, the losses on holding shares can be substantial. The rewards are that in the long term, at least for as long as there have been properly measured stockmarkets from which to judge, excess rewards have been earned from holding shares. In other words, risk diminishes with the passage of time.

The preceding discussion is based on inductive logic: that things will happen like this because that is the way they always have done; and that investors earn excess returns over bonds and inflation from holding equities because that is the way it always has been. However, there is a strong case for saying this is how it should be. Equities have a dynamic capability that is quite simply absent in bonds, whose nominal returns are fixed when they are issued. The only doubts affecting them are the extent to which inflation will erode these returns and the chances of the borrower defaulting.

Equities represent the risk capital that is invested in projects to produce the best return. Such capital can be, and is, reinvested elsewhere when better opportunities arise. This mobility can be overstated, yet in a world where risk capital is finite, demand for it will always draw it to where the returns are likely to be acceptable. The benchmark of acceptability, as set by competitive capital markets, is something better than that offered by low-risk investments such as bonds.

If it can be concluded that in the long term equities will always return more than both inflation and bonds, that even the lowest possible returns from a well-diversified selection of equities will achieve this target, and that even the worst possible returns from equities are acceptable, then there is no particular reason to fear the future. It also raises a tantalising question: is it worth making the effort to try to beat the market averages and, indeed, is it possible to do so? This is the subject of the next essay.

ARE EXCESS RETURNS THERE FOR THE TAKING?

"If you're so clever, how come I'm so rich?" This is a pertinent question, delivered in typically forthright style by Warren Buffett, arguably the most successful investor on the planet and probably the best-known as well. Mr Buffett, whose investment prowess has brought him a personal fortune valued at around $30 billion, addresses his question to the academics who have propounded the persuasive but elusive theory that it is impossible for a statistically significant number of investors consistently to beat the stockmarket averages. Persuasive because there is a substantial body of evidence to back up the so-called efficient market hypothesis. Elusive because, as we shall see, this theory is infuriatingly difficult to pin down.

It is easy to agree that if the efficient market hypothesis did not exist it would have to be invented. Too many factors point in its direction, none more than the striking inability of professional investors to raise the value of the funds they manage faster than the increase in the stockmarket indices that they use as a benchmark.

Professional failure

Take the table opposite, reproduced from the *Investors Chronicle*, which shows the performance of mutual funds in the UK, where they are known as unit trusts, over one, five and ten years to the end of February 1996. On these findings, professional investors, the people with the most resources and arguably the best qualifications, are singularly incapable of beating their benchmark, which in this case is the FTSE All-Share index of 900 shares listed in London.

For example, out of 134 unit trusts, which aim for a combination of capital growth and acceptable income, not one managed to beat the All-Share index in the year to February 1996. No winners out of 134 contestants is not impressive.

Performance over longer periods is almost as bad. Only two out of 79 trusts in this group with a ten-year history managed to beat the market over that period. The record of trusts with different investment goals is much the same.

How few unit trusts beat the market
(value of £100 invested)

	1 year	5 years	10 years
All-Share index	129	200	380
Average UK equity growth trust	121	175	277
No. of trusts in category	146	123	69
No. beating All-Share index	15	8	7
Average UK equity income trust	116	166	304
No. of trusts in category	82	72	55
No. beating All-Share index	1	2	6
Average UK growth & income trust	118	166	287
No. trusts in category	134	117	79
No. beating All-Share index	0	5	2

Nor, on the basis of these findings, can unit trust managers fall back on a familiar defence of their record: that their performance figures are cited after accounting for the charges they have to carry (the cost of dealing and management fees) whereas a market index is not burdened with such things. The average of the 134 "growth and income" trusts just mentioned added 18% to their value in the year to end-February, when the market rose 29%. Of that 11 percentage point gap between the two, about 6.5 points could reasonably be accounted for by charges. "The rest," as the *Investors Chronicle* put it, "is plain, simple failure." These findings are not unusual. Many similar surveys covering three decades of research in both the UK and the United States reveal the same pattern.

It gets worse. First, the small number of funds which do beat their benchmark over a particular period becomes even smaller when account is taken of the risks they bore. In other words, some supposedly winning funds comprised an above-average number of shares whose price, on the basis of past observations, had a propensity to exaggerate movements in the market. So when the market rose, assuming the past correlation remained true, these funds would rise faster.

Win some, lose others

The obverse of this is that when the market falls, the value of these funds would fall faster. This leads on to the second point: that there is little consistency among winning funds. Those which are leaders one year are likely to be laggards the following year.

For instance, in his investment classic, *A Random Walk Down Wall Street*, Burton Malkiel took the performance of the top 20 mutual funds for the period 1970–80 and found that only two of these – Fidelity's Magellan Fund and Twentieth Century Select – made it into the top 20 for 1980–90. Furthermore, for 1970–80 the average annual return for the top 20 was 19% compared with 10% for a group of 177 similar mutual funds. In 1980–90 the returns from the top 20 of the previous decade became quite ordinary: 11.1% per year compared with 11.7% for the average of similar funds, whose numbers by this time had grown to 309.

We have focused on the performance of mutual fund managers. Their chief failing is to have records that are publicly available and easily verifiable. There is nothing to suggest that they do any worse than the managers of other sorts of funds, such as closed-end funds, pension funds, and so on.

On one level this should be no surprise. After all, when aggregated, the value of all types of professionally managed funds is a substantial proportion of the value of the stockmarkets in which they invest. Effectively these funds are the market and clearly the market cannot beat itself.

How much skill, how much luck?

What is arguably a greater disappointment for those who aspire to do better than the market is the depressingly sparse number of investors who consistently achieve this. Although keen readers of *Barron's* might be able to name a couple of dozen investment superhitters, such as Warren Buffett, George Soros, John Neff and Michael Price, the truth is that there are no more of them than the laws of chance allow.

Even if it is clear that there are not enough superhitters to be statistically significant, that still leaves unanswered the question: why is this so? This is where the market's efficiency comes in. In large liquid markets, such as that for blue-chip shares in the UK and the United States, where information flows effortlessly and speedily and no single investor has the clout to influence the market unduly, no one can consistently gain a useful advantage. Thus betting on share prices, which is effectively what investors do, is no more scientific than betting on the toss of a coin, say efficient market theorists. Anyone can have a run of luck and guess correctly several times consecutively. A few can remain on such a roll that their good fortune becomes a form of genius. But when it comes down to it, it is pretty well impossible to prove that good luck is not the major factor at work here.

Market efficiency

It is worth noting, though, that if the market is efficient, then a paradox lies at the heart of its efficiency: it is only made efficient by the army of investment analysts and their employers who believe in its intrinsic inefficiency. In their unceasing efforts to sift every piece of investment information in search of nuggets that will bring them or their clients advantage – nuggets which, says the theory, cannot be found on any systematic basis – these analysts make the market efficient.

Not surprisingly, few professionals have much truck with efficient market hypothesis. It is hardly in their interests to do so. Warren Buffett himself derided the notion in an address he gave in 1984 to commemorate the 50th anniversary of the publication of *Security Analysis*, the investment textbook written by Benjamin Graham and David Dodd, which shaped so many of the tools of investment analysis with which thousands of analysts now work. "I am convinced there is much inefficiency in the market," he said. "When the price of a stock can be influenced by a 'herd' on Wall Street with prices set at the margin by the most emotional person, or the greediest person, or the most depressed person, it is hard to argue that the market always prices rationally. In fact, market prices are frequently nonsensical."

However, Benjamin Graham, Mr Buffett's mentor, a founding father of investment analysis and for many years an exceptional stock picker in his own right, eventually recanted. Shortly before his death in 1976 he said, in an interview with *Financial Analysts Journal*: "I am no longer an advocate of elaborate techniques of security analysis in order to find superior value opportunities. This was a rewarding activity, say, 40 years ago ... but the situation has changed. I doubt whether such extensive efforts will generate sufficiently superior selections to justify their cost ... I'm on the side of the 'efficient market' school of thought."

Truths, conundrums and irrationality

Yet for every piece of information in favour of the market's efficiency, there is a countervailing piece that contradicts it. Most obviously there are investment anomalies which consistently bring above-average returns and are consequently well known. Because they are so familiar, an efficient market should anticipate them and price them away, but they continue to occur.

The tendency for groups of stocks selling on a low multiple of their earnings to do better than those selling on a high multiple is one example. Studies in both the UK and the United States stretching back to the 1960s have revealed this phenomenon. The excess returns of low price/earnings (P/E) ratio stocks remain even after adjusting first for share-price volatility (stocks whose price movements exaggerate changes in the stockmarket of which they are a component will do better than those without this characteristic in rising markets) and second for the bias towards small companies among the low P/E ratio stocks. Investors might demand higher returns from small companies' shares than those of larger ones because their businesses are riskier.

Another is the size effect: that shares in companies with a small stockmarket capitalisation will do better than average. Here, too, evidence supporting this is found on both sides of the Atlantic and it holds good after adjusting for share-price volatility.

Possibly the most odd is the January effect: the tendency for stocks in companies with small market capitalisations to post exceptionally good returns in January. This can be rationalised away. In the United States, at any rate, small cap stocks are bought back in January at the start of the tax year having been sold in December to establish tax losses. But this does not explain why a market of competing investors allows it to persist.

In addition to the list of anomalies, there is plenty of evidence that investors do not price stocks rationally, which they should do in profit-maximising efficient markets. How else is it possible to explain big changes in market prices on the back of comparatively flimsy pieces of new information? For example, why did an increase in German interest rates in October 1987 cause the Dow Jones Industrial Average to fall 23% in a day? Either the index was overvalued in the first place or investors badly overreacted to the news.

Besides, controlled experiments have shown that people price risks badly. In the jargon, they are risk-seeking in the face of losses. Assume that a group of people each with $10,000 are given a choice: either they can keep just $2,000 of it; or they can take a 15% chance of keeping the $10,000 and an 85% chance of losing the lot. Most people will choose the 15/85% option. Yet this is the less valuable option of the two. The first must be worth $1,999, but the second is worth only $1,500.

A difficult game of choice

The argument could continue to swing to and fro. In the end it probably comes down to personal preference. That modern, liquid stockmarkets are highly efficient is not in doubt. But there is a crucial difference between accepting that shares are correctly priced most of the time and accepting that their prices are so close to perfection that it is not worth the effort to find the exceptions.

Indeed, these limitations are implied by the notions of weak, semi-strong and strong forms of market efficiency. Weak-form efficiency – that a stock's price history can have no effect on its future price – is widely accepted, except by technical analysts whose core belief is the opposite; that is, that price history can say something about the future.

Arguments for semi-strong efficiency – that all publicly known information about a stock is always factored into its price – and strong-form efficiency – that even inside information is priced into a stock – are less clear. Indeed, to the extent that the idea can be tested, the evidence indicates that strong-form efficiency does not exist. That is, those with truly privileged information, in particular a company's officers, can regularly turn it to their advantage.

However, it should be evident that beating the market consistently is a near-Herculean task. Mr Buffett exaggerates when he says that stock prices are too often set by the most depressed, greedy or emotional player in the market. This does happen, but for the most part they are set by clever, well-informed people with strong incentives to act sensibly.

The message therefore may be to try to beat the market if you can, but to come well equipped. What such equipment might comprise is dealt with next.

FIRST STEPS IN BUILDING A PORTFOLIO

You've got a lump of capital and you want to invest it to see if you can turn it into something more substantial. What should you do? Ask this question of any number of investment professionals and they will answer with one voice. "Diversification" is the mantra they will recite. Diversification is good, they will say. Diversification reduces risk. Diversification lets you sleep at night.

True enough, diversification – if used properly – is crucial. But would that it were that simple. Diversify by all means, but diversify from what? To explain, let's go back a step and pose another question: what is the point of investing capital in the first place?

For some the answer may be simply the thrill of the chase; the stimulus provided by competing in a global battle between the world's investors where the score is kept by the stockmarket indexes and there can be no doubt as to who are winners and who are losers. Such investors need read no further. This essay is not for them, though they may want to consider the essays "Investment dreams and reality" and "The lessons of the masters".

However, most investors will, at some stage, want to move from this gung-ho approach to something more considered. For them, the point of investing capital now is purely pragmatic. It is to build up a reserve of capital that can be turned into cash and used for consumption at various points and at various rates in the future.

Assess your future needs

The first step is to consider the needs for future consumption. When will capital need to be turned into cash and at what rate? Such questions do not have easy answers, but they can be answered approximately.

For example, at a simple level, imagine that someone decides that in 25 years' time he will need an annual investment income that is worth the inflation-adjusted equivalent of £20,000 today. How much capital will he need to generate that amount? First, assume that inflation averages 3% a year for the next 25 years, so the inflation-adjusted income would be £20,000 × $(1.03)^{25}$, which is £41,875. Next, assume that this income is paid from a lump of capital as a 6% annuity. How much capital is needed to generate a 6% return? The answer is almost £700,000. If our saver starts with £50,000 of capital, by what annual compound rate must that sum grow to become £700,000 by the due date? The answer is 11%. This is the compounding rate that turns £50,000 into £700,000 over 25 years. This rate of investment return is perfectly feasible if you assume that equity investment returns for the coming 25 years will be similar to those of the last 25.

In the real world, considerations are rarely so straightforward, but they move along similar lines. The key questions for savers are: "What will I need?" and "When will I need it?" It is only when these have been answered that savers can progress to the fundamental investment question: "How can I get it?"

It is self-evident that a given monetary target is easier to hit the lower the investment return needed to achieve it and the longer the time allowed to do it. From this truism investment styles will flow. Someone with a substantial amount of capital already built up and just a few more years of excess saving over consumption should take a cautious approach to further investment. Someone with little capital but a lot of time can afford to be more adventurous. Not so much because he or she has little to lose – this is not necessarily the case – but because there is plenty of time to absorb the blows that the investment markets periodically deal out and still make a satisfactory return.

Investment markets do indeed deal out blows, even if the success of the world's equity markets these past 20 years have dulled many investors to that sober truth. This is where the key word "diversification" comes in, as does its near opposite, "risk".

These words are the yin and yang of investment, the matter and anti-matter of the investment universe. Where you have more of one, you will have less of the other, says conventional wisdom. Conventional wisdom is right, but only up to a point. The trouble is that too little thought is given to precisely what is meant by risk and by diversification.

The meaning of risk

The *Oxford English Dictionary* defines risk as the "chance or possibility of a danger, loss or injury". For investment purposes, this has been translated to the "chance that the actual outcon : from an investment will differ from the expected outcome". Here "differ" does not just mean differ negatively, it also means differ positively. In other words, an investment can turn out to be better than expected and still be defined as risky.

This is because of the way that risk is quantified for investment purposes. Risk is almost always defined as the price volatility of the investment in question. An investment whose price has historically been volatile bounces around a lot, but it bounces up as well as down. However, the statistical formulae that are used to measure risk cannot distinguish between upward moves and downward moves. All they can do is quantify the degree of movement from an average and conclude that a lot of movement, whichever way, equals lots of risk; little movement equals little risk. There is some logic in this train of thought. But it is a shortcoming of the conventional investment process rather than a strength, and it drives an equally shaky investment conclusion: that the greater the price volatility of an investment the riskier it becomes within a portfolio, and, therefore, the more that such an investment should be treated cautiously and used sparingly within a portfolio.

Yet it is worth asking why because, as Robert H. Jeffrey, an American investment manager, once observed: "Portfolios feel no pain." In other words, a portfolio is only an abstract entity. It is, as discussed earlier, a means to an end, that end being to be able to generate cash as and when needed. If there is no need to generate cash at a particular time, it does not matter how queasy the portfolio may feel as a result of the bouncing motion of its risky components. The portfolio's state of health matters only if it cannot produce cash when required.

So investors can take a more liberal approach to risk within an investment portfolio than conventional wisdom would allow if they recognise that the risk that affects a portfolio's monthly valuations does not matter. What is important is the risk that affects a portfolio's cashflow.

The meaning of diversification

Diversification is said to reduce risk, but the more relaxed approach to risk suggested above makes that notion superfluous. This is because risk diversification too often leads to a Noah's Ark approach to investment: two of everything. To caricature the argument: it does not matter what the investment is, put it into your portfolio and it will reduce risk. But a fundamental conclusion of modern portfolio theory is that what counts is not diversification itself, but how you diversify.

Take, for example, the mix of equities and government bonds within a portfolio. Government bonds – gilts in the UK, Treasury bonds in the United States – are the definitive risk-free asset because the likelihood that the government will default on its obligations are effectively zero. Therefore, if both the interest and principal payments of a bond are guaranteed and the bond's term (the period until it is repaid) matches an investor's cashflow needs, then holding bonds within a portfolio brings no risk. On this logic, no investment professional dare suggest that a well-balanced portfolio can be without government bonds.

But this ignores the rule that it is how you diversify that really counts. Investment returns from equities and bonds usually move together. In the jargon of portfolio theory, they have a positive co-variance. This means that when shares go up, bonds generally go up too; and when shares fall, bonds usually follow suit. This should be no great surprise, since most of the big factors that affect share prices, most notably interest rates, also affect bonds. But it means that in a portfolio comprising mostly equities, bonds are not much good at reducing risk (risk here defined as the variability of returns). Furthermore, bonds have lower expected long-term returns than equities. So if bonds are not much good for hedging risk and carry a lower return than equities, the question arises: why bother to hold bonds at all?

The solution may be to hold cash as a portfolio's hedging instrument instead of bonds. Like bonds, cash invested in a savings account carries no risk of loss (other than through the corrosive effects of inflation). Unlike bonds, however, the correlation between the value of cash and the value of equities is weak or even negative. This is because the value of cash stands still regardless of whether equities go up or down. It is true that expected long-term returns are higher from bonds than from cash. True, but irrelevant, because we have already dismissed the idea of holding bonds within a portfolio because they are not much good at reducing the risks that come with holding equities. Therefore, cash becomes the only serious alternative.

But how much cash do investors need to hold in their investment portfolio? Probably less than they imagine. This because by the time they come to put an investment portfolio together, most people will have built up a substantial array of assets, including large amounts of cash sloshing around in various savings accounts. Such cash, however, is part of their overall wealth. So to reserve parts of their investment portfolio specifically for cash as a hedging instrument may be taking prudence too far to the detriment of their long-term cash-flow.

The same could be said for their other assets. Why, for example, would a house owner want to own shares in a house-building company when the factors that affect the value of one will affect the other in almost equal proportion? Similarly, why should an engineer want to hold shares in an engineering company when he already has a full exposure to that industry through the capitalised value of his future earnings from employment? The answer may be because he knows enough about the ins and outs of that industry to spot a good bargain when he sees one. But no one could argue that it is a good risk-hedging technique.

This essay is, of course, a generalisation. Every investment portfolio, if it is to do its job, must be unique because it will have unique needs to meet. That said, the three key questions posed hold good.

- What will I need?
- When will I need it?
- How can I get it?

If the getting is what investment is really about, then two generalisations hold good: diversify less, because you are already more diversified than you think; take more risk, because it is only the risk that affects your cashflow that matters.

INVESTMENT DREAMS AND REALITY

Never in the history of stockmarkets has so much value been given to so many companies making so little profit. In 2000 investors saw the proof of this statement everywhere they looked in the major stockmarkets of the United States and Europe.

Take the table below. It shows stockmarket values in April 2000 for eight high-technology companies that were beloved of investors (four each from the United States and the UK). These were hardly tiddlers. At that time, AOL was the 20th largest company in America, as measured by its stockmarket value, and Yahoo was in the top 50. All four of the UK entrants were in the FTSE-100 index of the UK's most valuable companies. Yet only four out of the eight had made a profit in their most recent financial year. The other four had made aggregate losses of $819m.

Company	Stockmarket value ($bn)	Net profit ($m)
US companies		
AOL	176.3	762
Yahoo	116.6	26
Amazon	27.9	−720
eBay	16.6	2
UK companies		
Colt Telecom	31.8	−89
ARM	12.2	11
Freeserve	8.4	−2
Baltimore Technologies	2.9	−8
Aggregate	**392.7**	**−18**

In 1999 these eight made aggregate net losses of $18m, yet they were valued at $393 billion on the US and UK stockmarkets. In contrast, the biggest US company by market value in April 2000 was General Electric, a diverse group whose interests are a mixture of old economy capital goods and financial services. General Electric's market value was a mighty $534 billion. Yet to generate this scale of value it had to produce $10,717m of net profit in 1999.

Clearly, the lack of profit in many technology companies did not deter investors from believing that they were most valuable. This might seem odd to anyone coming fresh to investment analysis, because one of the first principles that newcomers learn is that it is the quantity of profit that drives the value of a business. But it does not follow that where there is little profit *now*, there is little business value, because putting a value on the *future* is what stockmarkets and investment are all about. When the market said that Cisco Systems, which supplies infrastructure for the Internet, was the most valuable business in the United States with a worth of $533 billion (as it did in March 2000), what it really meant was that the value of all the future income (net of taxes and all other outgoings) that Cisco would ever generate for its shareholders was $533 billion, after allowing for all uncertainties.

Making such an assertion for Cisco, or indeed any company, is a big claim because there is no let-out clause. Certainly, the stockmarkets themselves can change their collective judgment as the uncertainties change. But any individual who accepts a value at a specific time, through buying or selling a stock at a specific price, cannot back out a week later by saying: "Well, I've reappraised the uncertainties and I think the value is now x." That individual is saddled with the transaction he or she made.

Overturning logic
This being so, logic would suggest that the companies that are the most valuable would be the ones where the uncertainties are least. And, in the matter of valuing companies, nothing minimises uncertainty like the existence of a fat bottom line on a company's income statement which says that it made a profit for the year in question. Because where there is a profit, there are earnings for shareholders and tangible figures for investors to grasp – figures that tell them what returns a

company made on its revenue and on the capital it employed.

In 2000, however, logic had been turned on its head in the equity markets of the developed economies. Where once there were profits to drive company valuations, Internet technology or, more precisely, dreams about Internet technology, had taken over the job. Dreams – exaggerated hopes, if you like – can be vitally important to stockmarkets. Writing in 1961, Walter Gutman, who wrote an influential Wall Street newsletter in the 1950s and 1960s, said: "There is a particular moment when the value of mystery is at its greatest. When everyone sees something amazing coming out of mystery … they will pay a lot more to know about this strange new thing. Because no wealth you will ever have will equal your dreams, stocks go to particularly high levels when a lot of people think that they might equal their dreams."

Mr Gutman could have been writing about Internet technology. The number of investors who fully understand the workings of microprocessing technology is small, so to most of them the technology is a mystery. Yet simultaneously the returns that many Internet stocks posted in 1998 and 1999 exceeded investors' wildest dreams.

Proof, if it were needed, comes in no neater form than that provided by Jay Ritter of the University of Florida, who for many years has logged the subsequent share price performance of companies that have been newly listed on US stock exchanges. In 1999 the vast majority of companies coming new to the US stock exchanges – especially the technology-oriented NASDAQ market – were Internet-related business, especially so-called dot.com companies, which are basically Internet billboards and retailers. Mr Ritter found that the share prices of 117 initial public offerings (IPOs) doubled on their first day of trading in 1999. In contrast, in the 25 years from 1974 to 1998 the share prices of just 39 IPOs doubled on their first day.

Further, in 1999 the average gain from first-day trading of the total 463 IPOs was 70%, whereas the average from first-day trading for the other nine years of the 1990s was 13.7%. Put another way, the aggregate gains on first-day trading to successful subscribers of ipos was $36 billion in 1999. For the years 1990–98, the aggregate gain was $27.6 billion.

Rationalising dreams

Dreams, however, must be rationalised, especially in investment analysis, whose cornerstone is the assumption that share prices are set by profit-seeking individuals acting logically. It can never allow that a business's stockmarket value is really a triumph of hope over common sense. Yet where a business is making no profit and has little likelihood of doing so in the near future, there is an obvious lack of material with which to build.

However, instead of focusing on profits, investment analysts quickly focused on the quantum of customer interest that Internet businesses were generating and related it to stockmarket value. Thus, for example, if Yahoo, the world's leading Internet search directory, attracts 26m visits per month to its site and has a stockmarket value of $32 billion, as it did in mid-1999, then its value per site visit was about $1,233.

In a sense, Yahoo must have a value per site visit, it is simply an arithmetical function of dividing two numbers, just as a retailer will have a value for every consumer who happens to wander past its shop window. The question is whether there is a useful correlation between wandering consumers and stockmarket value from which predictions of value can be made.

It may well be that the more web surfers an Internet portal attracts, the more valuable its potential becomes. So far, so good. However, it is a leap of logic – or, rather, of faith – to say, for example, that because Yahoo is worth $1,233 per site visit, then Alta Vista, another search engine, must be worth something similar; or, as happened in practice during 1999, that Alta Vista's shares are cheap because their value per site visit is only one-quarter that of Yahoo's.

The problem is that both assessments of company valuation are made with the company's value, as reckoned by the stockmarket, already an integral part of the calculation. This is not very helpful. It is just telling us that Alta Vista's shares are cheap if Yahoo's shares are cheap too. It does not begin to build a model where Yahoo's value is a product of the argument, rather than being part of the argument itself.

At least exercises in discounted cashflow (DCF) analysis do that. This is the modelling of what stockmarkets are supposed to be in the business of: putting a value on the future. DCF produces a figure, in today's money values, for all the future cashflow that a company will generate for its shareholders. The trouble is, the future is impossible to predict with certainty.

The uncertainties are magnified if the company being valued does not yet make profits. The exercise then involves making assumptions that will get the company into profit and more assumptions about the rate at which profits will grow. Assumptions beget doubts and doubts beget uncertainty. Theoretically, DCF can cope with this. It does so by changing the discount rate – the rate at which future figures are reduced to today's values. The greater the uncertainty, the higher is the discount rate, and the less is today's value of possible future profits.

It may be that DCF analysis is the least bad way of valuing complex business propositions that stretch out far into the future, although the valuations that it produces must be treated with extreme caution. Benjamin Graham in his 1973 book, *The Intelligent Investor*, said: "Many years ago we advised readers to buy their stocks as they bought their groceries, not as they bought their perfume. The really dreadful losses of the past few years were realised in common stock issues where the buyers forgot to ask 'How much?'."

But none of us, expert analysts included, is really much good at answering this question, the fault lying as much with the analysts themselves as with the analysis. A psychologist from Stanford

University, Amos Tversky, who widely researched people's responses to uncertainty, wrote about decision-making in investment management in 1995. He concluded that experts are "optimistic; they overestimate the chances that they will succeed and they overestimate their degree of knowledge in the sense that their confidence far exceeds their hit rate."

This may be a large part of the reason dream valuations arise in the first place, as well as the allure of "something amazing coming out of mystery", as noted by Walter Gutman back in 1961. Mr Gutman also knew that dreams are replaced by reality. He was writing about investors' love affair with computer stocks and he forecast: "When computers are as familiar as cash registers, IBM will sell at a much less romantic value – you wait and see." He wasn't far wrong. In the years 1962–63, IBM's share price fell from $607 to $300 in seven months.

LESSONS OF THE MASTERS

In any pursuit there are some people who bring genius to the activity in question. But genius, almost by definition, generally lies beyond the scope of analysis. This is not to say it cannot be analysed, but to question whether analysis will bring much benefit to those who aspire to emulate by way of imitation. You cannot play the tenor saxophone like Charlie Parker or tennis like John McEnroe simply because you have figured out how they did it.

With investing it is a bit different. At the margins of the distribution curve for investing ability there are players who could be described as geniuses, even if – on the evidence of the previous essay – we might wonder if they are not just supremely lucky. Their record almost inevitably attracts close scrutiny, so predictably what makes them tick has become the subject of a cottage industry of investment writing, although a good chunk of it seems to get bogged down in irrelevant detail.

Much is made, for example, of the fact that two undisputed masters, Warren Buffett and Sir John Templeton, both make a virtue out of operating well away from the hurly-burly of Manhattan; Mr Buffett in Omaha, Nebraska, and Sir John in the Bahamas. To generalise from this statistically insignificant coincidence, however, would be foolish. We might just as well focus on the idiosyncrasies of other outstanding investors. Is superior investment performance facilitated by going round the world on a motorcycle like Jim Rogers (George Soros's original partner in the Quantum Fund); or breakfasting every day on a concoction of canned soup like Philip Fisher, a San Francisco-based money manager best known for his investment standard, *Common Stocks and Uncommon Profits*?

Leaving flippancy aside, there are lessons to be learned from the masters which can bring benefit to lesser mortals. These can be summed up in simple headings that might constitute a checklist for success in most occupations.

Intellectual ability

Although it may not be a prerequisite for success in investment, it clearly helps to bring lots of intellectual horsepower to the subject. The most common characteristic of the 18 outstanding investors studied in *The Money Masters* and *The New Money Masters* by John Train is probably academic achievement. Some, such as Sir John Templeton and Michael Steinhardt, are outstanding academically; none were slouches.

Technical skills

These are too often taken for granted, yet they are crucial. For instance, the "how to do it" books written both about, or by, the masters pay too little attention to gathering the humdrum accountancy skills needed to understand a balance sheet. But without them, the idea that someone can buy shares with confidence is fanciful. The fact is that investment, as far as shares are concerned, is written about in the language of accountancy. It follows that an up-to-date understanding of accountancy is vital.

To some extent, the depth of understanding needed probably depends on the investment strategy that each investor adopts. Some demand intimate accountancy skills. To see shares as a businessman sees a whole company demands more than simply the ability to calculate basic accountancy ratios. It requires the knowledge and experience to assess qualitatively the profits that a company generates; to question, for example, whether they depend too much on capitalising expenses into the cost of inventory or offsetting charges against allowances already provided for.

This is the approach used by Warren Buffett, whose investment vehicle, Berkshire Hathaway, produced compound annual growth of 24% in net assets per share between 1965 and 1999, or Philip Fisher. Indeed, one chapter in Mr Fisher's *Common Stocks and Uncommon Profits* (What to Buy

– the 15 Points to look for in a Common Stock) poses the most demanding questions that any investor could ask. How do you address point 3: how effective are the company's research and development efforts in relation to its size? or point 10: how good are the company's cost analysis and accounting controls?

This prompts another question: for successful investing, is it better to know a lot about a little, or a little about a lot? Mr Buffett is clearly in the lot-about-a-little school. He makes a virtue out of knowing little about whole rafts of US industry. He has never owned a technology stock, for example. But, as he told "Adam Smith's Money World", a business TV programme: "I don't have to make money in every game. I mean, I don't know what cocoa beans are going to do. You know there are all sorts of things that I don't know about and that may be too bad. But why should I know about all of them?"

With Mr Buffett's record in selecting outstanding stocks from just a few industries it is difficult to quibble with this approach, but, in contrast, John Templeton, the founder of the Templeton Growth mutual fund, told his biographers: "I would part company with Buffett on this. I think you should try to understand companies, or you should hire someone who understands any company, any industry where there appears to be a good buy. It would be a mistake for someone to say: 'I am not going to buy high-tech stocks because I don't understand them.'" (*Global Investing, the Templeton Way*)

At the other end of the accounting spectrum, required knowledge of both individual companies and their accounting quirks need only be limited if the investment approach is largely quantitative; that is, selecting stocks simply because they meet specified numerical criteria.

This approach is epitomised by Benjamin Graham's "bargain issues", perhaps the most successful purely formulaic method of choosing shares yet devised. In the 1930s Mr Graham, who, incidentally, had an exceptional understanding of accountancy, devised a method the aim of which was to choose a diversified group of common stocks, all of which sold for less than the per share balance-sheet value of their current assets minus all claims on the business. In other words, the value of a company's current assets minus the combined value of its current liabilities, debt and provisions should be greater than the stockmarket value of the entire company.

In John Train's apt phrase, this was like "buying a furnished home for less than the price of the furniture". After all, in this exercise, the buyer pays nothing for the fixed assets of the business: the land, buildings, plant and equipment. Assuming that someone, somewhere will believe there is even a half-decent return to be made on those assets, then the stock's value must eventually rise.

At its extreme, this approach does not even require investors to know the names of the companies they are buying. All they need to know is that the stocks satisfy the quantitative criteria and that their activities are sufficiently diversified across a broad spectrum of industry as to eliminate business risk.

This is just the job for computing power, which is why Mr Graham's bargain issues, and similar approaches, are less successful now than they were in Mr Graham's day. In the jargon of the second essay ("Are excess returns there for the taking?"), the stockmarket has become efficient at pricing such anomalies, if not to the point of extinction then at least to the level of endangered species.

Not that today's outstanding investors have much time for efficient markets, as we also discovered in the second essay. Indeed, many of them have little truck with the whole paraphernalia of portfolio theory, the development of which is closely tied to the concept of market efficiency. For example, while discussing those investors who had been profoundly influenced by *Security Analysis*, the landmark textbook by Benjamin Graham and David Dodd, Mr Buffett told his audience: "Our Graham and Dodd investors, needless to say, do not discuss beta, the capital asset pricing model, or covariance in returns among securities. These are not subjects of any interest to them. In fact, most of them would have difficulty defining those terms. The investors simply focus on two variables: price and value."

Yet increasingly there is a class of investors for whom these terms mean much; who recognise, either intuitively or explicitly, that within some elements of portfolio theory there is the basis of a sound rationale for making sometimes exceptional returns. As a class, these investors are hedge fund managers. Individually, their best-known exponents are people like George Soros, whose Quantum Fund compounded its unit value by over 30% a year between 1969 and 1999, or Michael Steinhardt, who retired in 1996 having grown the assets of Steinhardt Partners by about 30% a year between 1967 and 1995.

Hedge funds realised that by gearing up – that is, borrowing to increase their exposure to a market – they could raise their returns as long as the market's returns were greater than the cost of borrowing. This much is fairly obvious, but it is also confirmed by portfolio theory, which says there is a positive correlation between risk and reward.

Portfolio theory also says that the risks and returns within a single portfolio stem largely from the overall risks and returns being offered by the market. From this, it follows that the returns which result from picking specific investments – stocks, currencies, or whatever – are a small part of the total.

For investors who want to maximise the returns from their own assessments this is a bit disappointing. It is better to eliminate the effects of the market and isolate the effects of their own judgments. The clever thing about hedge funds is that, by a combination of borrowing to gear up their returns and short selling of the market to which they are exposed, they can achieve this. The more they gear up in response to opportunities spotted, the greater they make their short positions, leaving their exposure to market volatility constant. Assuming (and this is a big assumption) that a hedge fund has done its job properly, it would pick up the benefit of any increase in the market value of its specific investment and would be protected in the event of a fall in the market by the profits on its short position.

From this comparatively simple starting point, a whole panoply of hedge fund strategies has evolved. Within the current context, however, the question is not whether hedge funds are successful, but whether they offer instruction from which average investors might benefit, as they probably would from conscientiously assimilating the lessons that, say, Messrs Graham, Templeton and Fisher offer.

At the extreme, the technical skills of George Soros on a binge of interlocking big-picture plays are dazzling but of little practical value. However, the more prosaic lesson from hedge funds – that risk can be controlled and it is done through derivatives – is most likely to trickle through to the players on the public parks.

The mental approach

Contrast the following two quotations: "As a student of human nature, I have always felt that a good speculator should be able to tell what a man will do with his money before he does." And: "By arguments, examples and exhortation, we hope to aid our readers to establish the proper mental and emotional attitudes towards their investment decisions … We hope to implant in the reader a tendency to measure or to quantify … The habit of relating what is paid to what is being offered is an invaluable trait in investment."

The first quote belongs to Bernard Baruch, a famous trader on the New York Stock Exchange in the first third of the 20th century, who vied with the likes of J.P. Morgan and Joseph Kennedy to make the smartest moves on the street. The second comes from Benjamin Graham's *The Intelligent Investor*, one of the most widely read books on investment ever published.

They encapsulate each end of the investing

spectrum. On the one hand there are investors as poker players, looking to trade off the hopes and fears of the market to make a turn; on the other hand there are investors as savers, knowing that investing only when the odds are stacked firmly in their favour combined with the wonders of compounding will bring satisfactory returns in the long run.

Both approaches have something to commend them, although it is obvious that Mr Graham's "good value" approach has more to offer an investor of limited resources. But even such a cautious approach has its difficulties, as Mr Graham acknowledged when he wrote that the investor's chief problem was likely to be himself. The continual urge to do something – anything – scuppers the best-laid investment plans.

"It was never my thinking that made big money for me. It was always my sitting. Men who can be right and sit tight are uncommon. I found it one of the hardest things to learn. But it is only after a stock operator has firmly grasped this that he can make big money." This quote would do justice to Warren Buffett at his most avuncular. Yet the author was Jesse Livermore, a contemporary of Messrs Baruch and Kennedy, who made and lost several fortunes in a frenzy of dealing before he killed himself. He would have known.

Part 2

A–Z

ACCRUALS CONCEPT

A basic idea on which company accounts are based: that cause and effect should be linked by matching the costs which are incurred in running a business with the resultant revenue earned (although not necessarily received in cash) in the same accounting period. The alternative would be to have a system of cataloguing the cash transactions of a business and calling the net result profit or loss. But in any one year this would be likely to distort the picture of the company's performance since many cash costs would be incurred or revenue generated in respect of pieces of work that span more than one accounting year.

ACCRUED INTEREST

The interest that has been earned on a BOND since its most recent DIVIDEND was paid. The market price for bonds ignores this element; it quotes the price of bonds "clean" of accrued interest. However, a buyer would have to pay for the interest that has accrued. Imagine a bond with a 10% COUPON. If it were quoted in the market at $125 120 days after the last dividend had been paid then, ignoring dealing costs, a buyer would have to pay $125 plus 120/365 of $10; that is, $128.29.

ACT

See ADVANCE CORPORATION TAX.

ADR

See AMERICAN DEPOSITARY RECEIPT.

ADVANCE CORPORATION TAX

A taxation system used by the UK government to take a slice of income from the dividends that companies paid to their shareholders. However, advance corporation tax (ACT) had a penal effect on UK-based companies that made most of their profits overseas and was abolished in April 1999. Thus companies no longer have to pay the government 25% of the amount of the dividend that they paid to their shareholders. Correspondingly, shareholders no longer receive a tax credit equal to the value of the ACT paid. The exception to this rule, however, is that private investors still get a small tax credit, equal to 11% of the dividend that they receive, which they can offset against their tax liability.

ADVANCE-DECLINE LINE
Also known as the breadth of market indicator, this plots the number of share prices that rise minus the number of share prices that fall over a specific period (usually a day or a week) for a given stockmarket average (the S&P 500 index, for example). Followers of TECHNICAL ANALYSIS use this to gauge the strength of a stockmarket. In particular, if the advance-decline line shows a negative return (that is, more shares fall than rise) yet the stockmarket index continues to rise, they see this as an indication that the market is weak and as a prelude to a fall in the index.

AIM
See ALTERNATIVE INVESTMENT MARKET.

ALL-SHARE INDEX
See FTSE ACTUARIES ALL-SHARE INDEX.

ALPHA
The term has two distinct uses within PORTFOLIO THEORY, although they are mathematically similar.

1 Within a simplified pricing model used to identify those portfolios of investments that deliver the best combination of RISK and return, alpha is used to describe the expected return from a security or a portfolio assuming that the return from the market is zero. Thus in this model the expected return for, say, an ORDINARY SHARE would be its alpha plus the market return leveraged by the share's sensitivity to market returns (its BETA). Here both alpha and beta are estimated based on comparison of the historical returns of the share and the market (see also SINGLE INDEX MODEL).
2 In measuring portfolio performance, alpha is

used to define to what extent a portfolio has done better or worse than it should have done, given the amount of RISK it held. If it is accepted that a portfolio's performance will (simply speaking) depend on market returns times the portfolio's sensitivity to the market, then alpha quantifies the extent to which the portfolio's return varies from its expected return. Thus it measures the extent to which the manager adds or erodes value.

ALTERNATIVE INVESTMENT MARKET

The LONDON STOCK EXCHANGE's junior market for small, fast-growing companies, launched in June 1995. Its progress to date has substantially exceeded expectations and at the end of March 2000 385 companies were quoted on the Alternative Investment Market (AIM) with a combined stockmarket value of £18 billion. The logic behind the AIM was to form a market with a minimum of regulation and spiced with tax breaks, thus creating a cheap means of raising risk capital for young companies. Regulation is carried out by approved advisers rather than the exchange itself; and the information that companies have to supply is minimal as is the number of shares that have to be made available for trading.

AMERICAN DEPOSITARY RECEIPT

Most US investors who own shares in foreign corporations do so via American depositary receipts (ADRs). There is nothing to stop them buying overseas shares directly (although they may technically infringe the 1933 Securities Act when they come to sell them). ADRs, however, are much more convenient. Basically, they are tradable receipts which say that the underlying shares represented by the ADRs are held on deposit by a bank in the corporation's home country. The depository bank collects dividends, pays local taxes and distributes them converted into dollars. Additionally, holders of ADRs usually have all the rights of shareholders who own their STOCK directly. The vast majority of overseas corporations that list their shares on a US exchange use ADRs; at the end of

1999 there were over 1,000 such listings. ADRS have spawned imitators and nowadays there are global depositary receipts, basically ADRS which are traded on OVER-THE-COUNTER markets in both the United States and the EUROMARKET, and European depositary receipts, which are tracked on the PARIS BOURSE and FRANKFURT STOCK EXCHANGE.

AMERICAN STOCK EXCHANGE
Similar to the much bigger NEW YORK STOCK EXCHANGE (NYSE) in its organisation and trading arrangements, the American Stock Exchange (AMEX) has been squeezed by both the NYSE and NASDAQ and, indeed, was taken over by NASDAQ in 1998, although it continues to run independently. Its origins date back to street trading in the 19th century, and it was not until 1921 that it moved to a permanent building in Trinity Place in New York's financial district. By the mid-1960s the volume of stocks traded on AMEX reached half the level of business done on the NYSE. Since then, its relative importance has declined and at the end of 1999 902 US company securities were listed on AMEX with a combined market value of $142 billion. The comparative figures for the NYSE were 3,025 issues and market value of $12,296 billion.

AMORTISATION
US terminology for DEPRECIATION. In the UK amortisation generally refers to writing off the cost of INTANGIBLE ASSETS.

ANNUITY
An annual sum paid in perpetuity, usually for a fixed amount, although it can be linked to an index.

APT
See ARBITRAGE PRICING THEORY.

ARBITRAGE
To arbitrage is to make a profit without RISK and, therefore, with no net outlay of capital. In practical terms it requires an arbitrager simultaneously

to buy and sell the same ASSET – or, more likely, two bundles of assets that amount to the same – and pocket the difference. Before financial markets were truly global, arbitraging was most readily identified with selling a currency in one financial centre and buying it more cheaply in another. The game has now moved on a little, but, for example, there would be the potential to make risk-free profits if dollar interest rates were sufficiently high to allow traders to swap their euros for dollars and be left with extra income after they had covered the cost of their currency insurance by selling dollars forward in the FUTURES market. Similarly, arbitrage opportunities can be exploited by replicating the features of a portfolio of shares through a combination of EQUITY futures and bonds then simultaneously selling the actual stocks in the market. (See RISK ARBITRAGE.)

ARBITRAGE PRICING THEORY

A theory which aims to estimate returns and, by implication, the correct prices of investments. Intellectually, it is an extension of the CAPITAL ASSET PRICING MODEL. It says that the CAP-M is inadequate because it assumes that only one factor – the market – determines the price of an investment, whereas common sense tells us that several factors will have a major impact on its price in the long term. Put those factors into a model and you are making progress.

Thus arbitrage pricing theory (APT) defines expected returns on, say, an ORDINARY SHARE as the RISK-FREE RATE OF RETURN plus the sum of the share's sensitivity to a variety of independent factors. (Here sensitivity, as with the CAP-M, is defined by the share's BETA.) The problem is to identify which factors to choose. This difficulty is not helped by the fact that academic studies have come up with varying conclusions about the number and identity of the key factors, although benchmarks for interest rates, inflation, industrial activity and exchange rates loom large in tests.

In practical terms the aim of using APT would be simultaneously to buy and sell a range of shares whose sensitivity to the chosen factors was such that a profit could be made while all exposure to the effect of the key variables and all capital outlay were cancelled out. To the extent that APT assumes that markets always seek equilibrium, it says that the market would rapidly price away such ARBITRAGE profits.

Alternatively, a portfolio could be chosen which could be expected to outperform the market if there were unexpected changes in one or more key factors used in the model, say industrial activity and interest rates. As such, however, that would be doing little more than betting on changes in industrial production and interest rates and would not have much to do with minimising RISK for a given return. Resolving problems such as these means that APT gives greater cause for thought to academics than to investors.

ARITHMETIC MEAN

The full term for what non-mathematicians intuitively call the average and which is generally shortened simply to the mean. It is calculated by taking the sum of a series of values and dividing that number by the number of values. So if 12 values add up to 96, the average is eight. It should not be confused with the GEOMETRIC MEAN, under which heading there is a fuller discussion of the circumstances in which it is more appropriate to use one or the other.

ASSET

For something so fundamental to investment the surprise is that the definition of an asset is so vague. The US accounting standards body has defined it as being "probable future economic benefits obtained or controlled by a particular entity as a result of past transactions or events". However, within the context of a company's BALANCE SHEET, an asset is also a deferred cost. If a company shows plant and equipment of £1m in its balance sheet then that represents past expenditures which have yet to be written off and which, according to the ACCRUALS CONCEPT of accounting, will be depreciated as the plant is used up. The test of whether the plant is ultimately an asset or a liability will be whether it generates after-tax revenue greater than its cost. For a company to survive, most plant and equipment must pass that test. But for other items which are carried forward as assets, such as the deferred cost of a pension fund, there is no question that they can bring economic benefits.

More generally, the broad categories of investments within a portfolio – shares, bonds, property – are known as assets. Hence the term ASSET ALLOCATION.

ASSET ALLOCATION

The process of deciding in which sorts of assets to make investments and what proportion of total capital available should be allocated to each choice. The task is as relevant to private investors as it is to giant savings institutions. The latter formalise the process rather more, however, often beginning with a "top down" approach, which decides both in which ASSET classes to make investments (shares, bonds, real estate, cash, other classes) and in which geographical areas to invest (North America, Europe, East Asia, emerging markets, for example). Estimates of the likely returns from individual investment choices combined with the target return that the institution seeks will drive the selection process. From this will follow the decision to invest an above-average or below-average proportion of funds in some markets with reference to benchmark weightings that are commercially available.

ASSET STRIPPING

The term first coined in the UK in the late 1960s to describe the practice of taking over a company, splitting it into parts and selling them for a profit. It was a derogatory label since it implied no effort on the part of the acquirer to develop the company. By the late 1980s asset stripping was more in tune with the spirit of the times, so when the practice once more swept through the corporations of the UK and the United States it was more likely to be called "financial restructuring".

> *The key to a successful portfolio is proper management of your assets and stripping should be left to wallpaper products.*
> Jim Slater

BACKWARDATION

In a FUTURES market the price of a contract for future delivery of, say, a commodity usually trades above the SPOT PRICE because the notional interest received from holding cash rather than the underlying commodity is added to the cost of the contract. Sometimes, however, demand for the commodity pushes the spot price above the futures price. This is a backwardation, also known as an inverted market.

BALANCE SHEET

The financial statement of what a company owns and what it owes at a particular date. Traditionally, the left-hand side of the balance sheet is a schedule of the company's assets (land, buildings, plant and equipment, cash and inventories); the right-hand side is a statement of the liabilities, either real or potential. Real liabilities comprise the debts the company must pay, that is, payables, plus its loans. Potential liabilities are the allowances that are likely to be paid: deferred taxes and, increasingly, post-retirement benefits for employees. The remaining item on the right-hand side is the shareholders' interest in the business. This is technically not a liability at all, but a statement of the RISK capital subscribed to the business adjusted by the aggregate of retained EARNINGS and (possibly) revaluation of some assets. The following example is a potted version of a company's balance sheet.

Assets ($ billion)		Liabilities ($ billion)	
Properties, land, equipment	19.6	Short-term debt	2.7
		Long-term debt	13.1
Intangible assets	19.3	Allowances	8.0
Inventories & cash	14.9	Deferred taxes	3.7
		Other liabilities	12.3
		Stockholders' equity	14.0
	53.8		**53.8**

BAR CHART

The most common type of price chart used to

identify patterns that may give clues to future price movements in the investment under scrutiny. Price is plotted vertically and time horizontally. The price change for each unit of time – day, week, month, and so on – is plotted by a vertical bar, the top and bottom representing the high and low respectively for each period. Usually there will be a horizontal tick attached to the bar, representing the closing price. On the bottom of the chart more bars sometimes plot the volume of business transacted, scaled to the right-hand axis. This helps correlate price changes to volume of business done, which may be significant. For example, a surge in the price of a share to new highs based on little volume could be a sign of impending weakness or, alternatively, a sign of strength if the buying has been done by informed insiders.

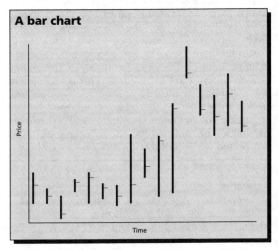

A bar chart

Price

Time

BARGAIN ISSUE

The Holy Grail for followers of VALUE INVESTING. The term has a general meaning indicating good value in an ORDINARY SHARE. However, through the writing of BENJAMIN GRAHAM, it also has a specific meaning which was successfully applied by Mr Graham and continues to be used by orthodox value investors, although usually with some modifications. These allow for the fact that stockmarkets are now generally more highly valued than when Mr Graham was working from the 1930s to the 1970s.

The specific meaning is that a bargain issue is when a company's ordinary shares sell in the market for less than the per share book value of current assets after deducting all other claims on the business. In other words, take a company's current assets (inventories, debtors, cash) and deduct not only the current liabilities (creditors, short-term borrowings) but also the long-term borrowings and any other allowances. The net result is that the shares of such companies sell for less than the value of net current assets with any fixed assets thrown in for nothing. Mr Graham found that buying a selection of such shares across a variety of industries invariably produced good investment returns.

BASIS

In a FUTURES market, basis is defined as the cash price (or SPOT PRICE) of whatever is being traded minus its futures price for the contract in question. It is important because changes in the relationship between cash and futures prices affect the value of using futures as a HEDGE. A hedge, however, will always reduce RISK as long as the VOLATILITY of the basis is less than the volatility of the price of whatever is being hedged.

BASIS POINT

One hundredth of a percentage point. Basis points are used in currency and BOND markets where the sizes of trades mean that large amounts of money can change hands on small price movements. Thus if the yield on a TREASURY BILL rose from 5.25% to 5.33%, the change would have been eight basis points.

BEAR

Someone who acts on the assumption that the price of a security in which he deals will fall. The origin is unknown, although it was common in

London by the time of the SOUTH SEA BUBBLE (1720). It probably derives from the occupation of a bear-skin jobber, about whom the saying went: "He's sold the bear's skin before he's caught the bear."

BEAR SQUEEZE

If too many speculators simultaneously sell STOCK they do not own in the hope of buying it back more cheaply later for a profit, they risk getting caught in a bear squeeze. The dealers from whom they must eventually buy stock to settle their obligations raise prices against them. When the bears scramble for stock to limit their losses they push up prices still further.

BEARER SECURITY

A security for which evidence of ownership is provided by possession of the security's certificate. The issuer keeps no record of ownership. A EUROBOND is generally issued in bearer form. It was common for the US Treasury and municipal authorities to issue bearer bonds too. However, in order to combat money laundering this was made illegal in 1983.

Invest in companies whose chairman is less than 5'8" tall.

Nigel Lawson, former UK chancellor of the exchequer

BELLWETHER STOCK

Just as the bellwether sheep is the one in the flock that all the others follow, so a bellwether STOCK is the one that is supposed to lead a market. It follows, therefore, that such stocks will be the ones with a big capitalisation, which can also reflect signs of which way the economies in which they trade are heading. In the UK Vodafone and BP Amoco fulfil this role as do, for example, Microsoft, General Motors and General Electric in the United States and Mitsubishi and Nippon Steel in Japan.

B

BETA

A widely used statistic which measures the sensitivity of the price of an investment to movements in an underlying market. In other words, beta measures an investment's price VOLATILITY, which is a substitute for its RISK. The important point to grasp is that beta is a relative, not an absolute, measure of risk. In stockmarket terms, it defines the relationship between the returns on a share relative to the market's returns (the most commonly used absolute measure of risk is STANDARD DEVIATION). But in so far as much of PORTFOLIO THEORY says that a share's returns will be driven by its sensitivity to market returns, then beta is a key determinant of value in price models for share or portfolio returns.

Although the mathematics involved in calculating beta are fairly complex, the end result is easy to understand. An investment's beta is expressed as a ratio of the market's beta, which is always 1.0. Therefore a share with a beta of 1.5 would be expected to rise 15% when the market goes up 10% and fall 15% when the market drops 10%. In technical terms, the beta is the coefficient that defines the slope of the regression line on a chart measuring the relative returns of a share and its underlying market. However, the beta values derived from the regression calculation can vary tremendously depending on the data used. A share's beta generated from weekly returns over, say, one year might be very different from the beta produced from monthly returns over five years.

This highlights a major weakness of beta: that it is not good at predicting future price volatility based on past performance. This is certainly true of individual shares. For portfolios of shares beta works far better, basically because the effects of erratically changing betas on individual shares generally cancel each other out in a portfolio. Also, to the extent that portfolio theory is all about reducing risk through aggregating investments, beta remains a useful tool in price modelling.

BID PRICE

The price that a dealer will pay for securities in the market. Thus it is the lower of the two prices that the dealer will quote for any security. For a MUTUAL FUND, it is the price at which the fund management company will buy in units from investors. (See also OFFER PRICE and SPREAD.)

BIG BANG

The event that took place on October 27th 1986 and transformed the way in which the LONDON STOCK EXCHANGE operated. It resulted from a deal between the government and the stock exchange in which the government dropped moves to challenge the exchange's restrictive practices in return for various liberalisation measures.

- The exchange scrapped the obligations that its members had to be either wholesalers of shares (jobbers) or brokers who dealt directly with investors.
- Brokers became free to supply clients with shares held in their own account and they could, if they wished, become market makers in shares.
- Restrictions on ownership of exchange member firms were first relaxed and then dropped, unleashing a flood of money into London as various financial conglomerates bought London jobbing and broking firms.
- A screen-based system of trading stocks (STOCK EXCHANGE AUTOMATED QUOTATIONS – SEAQ) closely modelled on the NASDAQ system was introduced, leading to the demise of floor trading on the exchange.

The abolition of exchange controls by the UK government in 1979 made these moves almost inevitable. The London market had to adapt to the globalisation of share trading or it would have become a backwater.

BINOMIAL OPTION PRICING MODEL

The basic principle behind this and other OPTION

pricing models is that an option to buy or sell a specific STOCK can be replicated by holding a combination of the underlying stock and cash borrowed or lent. The idea is that the cash and security combined can be fairly accurately estimated and their combined value must equal the value of the option. This has to be so, otherwise there would be the opportunity to make RISK-free profits by switching between the two.

Take a simple example, the aim of which is to find the value today of a CALL OPTION on a COMMON STOCK that expires in one year's time. The current stock price is $100, as is the call's EXERCISE PRICE. Now, to maintain clarity and avoid the complicating effect of an option's DELTA on the arithmetic involved, imagine that an investor holds just half of this stock (that is, $50-worth) in his portfolio. The portfolio's only other component is a SHORT position in a ZERO-COUPON BOND currently worth $42.45, which has to be repaid at $45 in a year's time.

Next assume that the value of the stock in a year's time will be either $110 or $90. From these two postulated outcomes several conclusions arise. First, we can value the call option in a year's time. It will be either $10 or zero. Second, we can value the portfolio. It too will be either $10 or zero. This must be so, since the value of the portfolio is the stock's value minus the debt on the zero-coupon bond. So it is either $55 minus $45, or $45 minus $45. The future value of the stock may be uncertain, but the value of the debt on the bond is not. Third, the alternative values for both the call option and the portfolio at the year end are the same. If this is so, then their start value must be the same as well. The start value for the portfolio can be easily calculated. It is $50 minus $42.45; that is, $7.55. So this must also be the present value of the call option.

From this basic building block of the binomial model comes the formula that the value of a call will be the current value of the stock in question multiplied by the option's delta (which, in effect, was 0.5 in our example) minus the borrowing needed to replicate the option. Using our example, the linear representation would be:

Call value = ($100 × 0.5) − $42.45 = $7.55

This is the single-period binomial model, so called because the starting point is to take two permitted outcomes for the stock price and then work back to find what this means for the present value of the option.

In the real world, however, a single-period model is not practical, hence the development of the multi-period binomial model where each period used to estimate the price of the option can be as short as computer power will allow. As the number of price outcomes rises by 2 to the power of the number of periods under review, the model is computer-intensive; a model using 20 periods, for example, would need over 1m calculations. Additionally, rather than using arbitrary stock-price outcomes from which to estimate the value of the option, the model takes advantage of the fact that, given an estimate of the rate at which a stock price will change, future stock prices can be estimated within a reasonable band of certainty using mathematical distribution tables.

The result is a model which produces options prices that closely mirror market prices. Furthermore, because the binomial model splits its calculations into tiny time portions, it can easily cope with the effect of dividends on stock prices and, hence, option values. This is an important factor with which the more widely used BLACK-SCHOLES OPTION PRICING MODEL copes less capably.

BLACK MONDAY

Monday October 19th 1987 when Wall Street had its worst day since 1914. The DOW JONES INDUSTRIAL AVERAGE fell 508 points from 2,247 to 1,738, or 22.6%. This triggered panic selling in EQUITY markets around the world and, for example, on the same day the UK's ALL-SHARE INDEX fell 9.7% from 1,190 to 1,075, then dropped a further 11% the following day. Until that point 1987 had been a great year for equities. From the start of the year until its mid-August peak, the Dow rose 44%. However, rising interest rates caused investors to worry and the decision of the German Bundesbank to increase its rates on October 16th was the cue for investors to dash for the exit.

The Dow bounced back rapidly from its low. On October 26th alone it put on 10%. The UK index, however, continued to fall and did not bottom out until December 3rd when it closed at 750, 39% below its mid-year peak.

Men, it has been well said, think in herds; it will be seen that they go mad in herds while they only recover their senses slowly and one by one.
Charles Mackay,
Extraordinary Popular Delusions and the Madness of Crowds

BLACK-SCHOLES OPTION PRICING MODEL

A pricing model that ranks among the most influential. It was devised by two Chicago academics, Fischer Black and Myron Scholes, in 1973, the year that formalised options trading began on the CHICAGO BOARD OF TRADE. The Black-Scholes model, or adaptations of it, has gained universal acceptance for pricing options because its results are almost as good as those achieved by other options pricing models without the complexity.

Behind the model is the assumption that ASSET prices must adjust to prevent ARBITRAGE between various combinations of options and cash on the one hand and the actual asset on the other. Additionally, there are specific minimum and maximum values for an OPTION which are easily observable. Assuming, for example, that it is a CALL OPTION then its maximum value must be the share price. Even if the EXERCISE PRICE is zero, no one is going to pay more than the share price simply to acquire the right to buy the shares. The minimum value, meanwhile, will be the difference between the share's price and the option's exercise price adjusted to its present value.

The model puts these fairly easy assumptions

into a formula and then adjusts it to account for other relevant factors.

- The cost of money, because buying an option instead of the underlying STOCK saves money and, therefore, makes the option increasingly valuable the higher interest rates go.
- The time until the option expires, because the longer the period, the more valuable the option becomes since the option holder has more time in which to make a profit.
- The VOLATILITY of the underlying share price, because the more it is likely to bounce around, the greater chance the option holder has to make a profit.

Of these, volatility, as measured by the STANDARD DEVIATION of share returns, is the most significant factor. Yet it was the factor over which Messrs Black and Scholes struggled because it is not intuitively obvious that greater volatility should equal greater value. That it is so is because of the peculiar nature of options: they peg losses to the amount paid for the option, yet they offer unlimited potential for profit.

Note that the basic Black-Scholes model is for pricing a call option, but it can be readily adapted for pricing a PUT OPTION. It also ignores the effect on the price of the option of any dividends that are paid on the shares during the period until the option expires. This is remedied either by deducting the likely present value of any DIVIDEND from the share price that is input into the model, or by using a refinement of the Black-Scholes model which writes off the effect of the dividend evenly over the period until it is paid.

BOLLINGER BANDS

Used in TECHNICAL ANALYSIS to determine areas of support for and resistance to price changes. On a chart these plot the STANDARD DEVIATION of the moving average of a price. So when they are plotted above and below the moving average, the bands widen and narrow according to the under-lying VOLATILITY of the average. The longer the period of low volatility, the closer together the lines become and the greater is the likelihood that there will be a break-out from the established price pattern.

BOND
Generic name for a tradable, long-term debt raised by a borrower who agrees to make specific payments, usually regular payments of interest and repayment of principal on maturity. (See also TREASURY BOND, EUROBOND, GILT-EDGED STOCK.)

BOND RATING
The chances that bonds of all types might go into default – that is, the borrower will fail to pay the interest and/or the capital due on a BOND – is rated by several credit organisations, the best known of which are Moody's and Standard & Poor's (S&P). Both organisations use a similar system to rate the safety of a bond, primarily based on a detailed ex-amination of the creditworthiness of the borrower and the terms of the bond. For S&P the credit rank-ings range from AAA (the best) to D, meaning that the bond is already in default. The Moody's ratings go from Aaa to D. However, only bonds with a rating of BBB or better (Baa in the case of Moody's) are considered "investment grade", that is, good enough for institutional investors. Bonds below these grades are colloquially termed junk bonds.

Both S&P's and Moody's bond ratings are moni-tored closely by investors and therefore any change in an issuer's ratings will be matched by a corre-sponding movement in the market price of its debt.

BONUS ISSUE
A misleading euphemism for a CAPITALISATION ISSUE.

BOOK VALUE
That part of a company's assets which belongs to its shareholders; in the UK these are generally known as shareholders' funds or, simply, net

assets. It is an accounting valuation arrived at by taking the gross assets of the business as shown in its BALANCE SHEET and subtracting all the prior claims on the business, such as bank debt, payables, allowances for future claims, and so on. Alternatively, it is the sum of the shares outstanding, additional paid-in capital and retained EARNINGS. Book value is usually expressed in per share terms so as to make an easy comparison with the market price of the shares (see PRICE TO BOOK RATIO).

BOTTOM FISHING
What value-seeking investors do after a stockmarket has fallen heavily, exposing good value in shares which fair-weather investors are still too shell-shocked to take.

BRADY BOND
Named after an American Treasury secretary, Nicholas Brady, who in 1989 came up with the Brady Plan to ease the debt burden that was crushing too many developing-country economies. Brady bonds are issued by indebted governments as part of a refinancing of their bank debt following the introduction of an agreed schedule between them and their creditors. This would be likely to include the adoption of responsible monetary policies by the governments concerned and some debt write-off by their bank lenders. Even so, Brady bonds, which are traded on OVER-THE-COUNTER markets, are high-RISK investments.

WARREN BUFFETT
Arguably the best-known investor on the planet. Mr Buffett is known for the world-class returns he has produced for over 30 years from his investment conglomerate, Berkshire Hathaway, and for his witty and insightful chairman's letter in Berkshire's annual report. Adding in the investment record of Mr Buffett's partnership, which he ran from 1956 to 1968 before sinking his capital into Berkshire, then his record from 1956 to 1999 showed an annual compound growth rate of

25.8%, enough to turn $1,000 into $19m. Over the same period, the pre-tax return from the S&P 500 index was 11.2% a year.

Mr Buffett is characterised as an exponent of VALUE INVESTING and he learned his trade from BENJAMIN GRAHAM, who first espoused that particular cause. In many respects, however, Mr Buffett's investment style is far removed from Mr Graham's. It focuses on the "business franchise", the idea that there is a small cadre of exceptional businesses whose advantages mean that they are protected from everyday economics. Brand-name corporations, or those which can grow on the back of bigger corporations – "gross royalty businesses" such as advertising agencies – are good examples.

BULL

An optimist; someone who assumes that prices will rise. The origin is unknown, although it probably evolved because it contrasts strongly with BEAR. As the quote from Alexander Pope shows, it was in common usage in London by the early 18th century.

> *Come fill the South Sea goblet full;*
> *The Gods shall of our stock take care:*
> *Europa pleased accepts the bull,*
> *And Jove with joy puts off the bear.*
> Alexander Pope, inscription on a punch bowl,
> 1720 (the year of the South Sea Bubble)

BULLETIN BOARD

A website where investors post gossip, fact and opinion about stocks and markets. Bulletin boards are immensely popular, but – given their virtual anonymity and their lack of regulation – they can be traps for unwary investors.

CAC 40 INDEX

The most widely quoted measure of share prices on the PARIS BOURSE. The CAC 40 (CAC stands for Compagnie Nationale des Agents de Change) was specifically developed as an index on which derivatives products could be based. It was introduced in 1988 with a base value of 1,000 for December 31st 1987 and comprises 40 of the 100 major stocks listed on France's monthly settlement market. During trading hours it is recalculated every time the price of one of its components changes.

CALENDAR EFFECT

Ostensibly there is little logic to the idea that some times of the year, or even days of the week, should be better times to trade shares than others. Even so, many studies have noted clear patterns of calendar bias to share returns. The best known ones are:

- **JANUARY EFFECT.** (See entry.)
- **Weekend effect.** Share prices tend to rise on Friday and fall on Monday.
- **Public holidays.** Like the weekend effect, shares tend to be stronger than average immediately before a public holiday (although not in the UK, according to one study).
- **Seasonal effects.** In the UK the months December–April tend to produce above-average returns and May–November below average, giving some credibility to the stockmarket saw: "Sell in May and go away."

October. This is one of the peculiarly dangerous months to speculate in stocks in. The others are July, January, September, April, November, May, March, June, December, August and February.
Mark Twain, *Pudd'nhead Wilson*

CALL HEDGE

A strategy in options trading which protects a

share or a portfolio against possible falls in market value. If an investor who holds a share, the price of which has risen substantially, fears for the share's short-term outlook he may HEDGE (that is, insure) his position by writing a CALL OPTION against the share. Thus the investor would receive an underwriting fee. If the share's price subsequently falls this would cover some or all of the losses sustained, depending on how thoroughly he had hedged his position. If, however, the share continues to rise the investor would have to cancel his obligation to deliver shares by buying a matching call. He would make a loss on that transaction, but would still participate in the rise of the underlying STOCK.

CALL OPTION

A call is the right to buy an ASSET, probably an ORDINARY SHARE, for a specific price usually within a specified period, although just on a specific date if it is a "European-style" option.

To give a simple example, ignoring dealing costs, say an investor is bullish about the prospects for a particular share and buys a call option contract for 20p giving him the right to buy the share at 380p. Assume also that the market price of the share is 350p. If and when the share price rises above 400p the investor is in profit, having covered his 20p option price and 380p EXERCISE PRICE. Although the price of the option will not actually move penny for penny with the price of the share, it will add considerable LEVERAGE to his speculation. If the share trades at 450p when the contract expires then the investor would have made 50p for an outlay of 20p, a 150% profit. If, instead, the investor had bought the share for 350p, his profit would have been 100p, or 29%. Alternatively, the investor would lose money if the share price is less than 400p when the contract expires, and he would lose 100% of his cost if it is less than 380p. His maximum losses, however, are always pegged at 20p. Whereas if he bought the share at 350p and it fell to 300p his losses would be 50p, although only 14% in percentage terms.

CAPITAL ASSET PRICING MODEL

Because of its comparative simplicity, the capital asset pricing model (CAP-M) is an influential formula for modelling the theoretically correct price of assets and portfolios. It developed out of PORTFOLIO THEORY in the 1960s, and, although the substantial body of academic research into its effectiveness increasingly draws critical conclusions, it remains an elegant theory which poses important questions about the extent to which investors can generate above-average returns from most investment selection techniques.

Basically, the CAP-M says that the return from an investment will equal the RISK-FREE RATE OF RETURN plus the excess return over the risk-free rate offered by the particular market in which the investment trades, in turn geared up by the sensitivity of the investment to market returns. For example, assume that the risk-free rate of return is 8% per year, that the market's return is 12% and that we are pricing a share whose sensitivity to the market is 1.2 times (that is, its historical returns have been 1.2 times whatever the market has done). The CAP-M would say that the share should return 12.8%; (the calculation is $8 + 1.2 [12 - 8]$).

If this exercise were repeated for a variety of shares or portfolios of differing VOLATILITY in relation to the market, a line on a chart could be drawn showing the trade-off between return and volatility, which is known as the SECURITY MARKET LINE. If the line shows expected future returns it would slope upwards, indicating that as RISK (substituted here by volatility) increased, so investors would expect higher returns for their outlay.

This can be useful for testing whether some investments are cheap or expensive. Say that a share's expected risk/reward trade-off put it at a point above the security market line. It would be offering excess returns for a given level of risk and would, theoretically, be bought till the returns it offered all future buyers were driven down to the market line. For a share which lay below the line the reverse would be true and it would be sold till its expected returns rose to the market line.

Note that there are just three components in the formula and two of these – the risk-free return and the market's return – are the same for a given period whatever investments are being priced. The only variable factor in the equation, and thus a crucial one, is the sensitivity of the particular investment's returns to those of the market. This is measured by the investment's BETA. Suffice it to say here that beta is a flawed measure, which may give decent indications of the sensitivity for a portfolio of many investments, but which says little about the likely price volatility of a single security.

This only partially undermines the credibility of the CAP-M as a way of modelling prices. Exhaustive testing of the CAP-M using historical price data shows that investors were rewarded for holding securities which have above-average sensitivity to the market, even if they were not as well rewarded as the theory suggests they should have been. In addition, the failings of the CAP-M are not sufficiently great to confound the theory that investors are almost solely rewarded for assuming the risk that they cannot diversify away (that is, market or SYSTEMATIC RISK) and that, therefore, taking on diversifiable risk (UNSYSTEMATIC RISK) brings no obvious benefits.

The determination of the value of an item must not be based on its price, but rather on the utility that it yields. The price for the item is dependent only on the thing itself and is equal for everyone; the utility, however, is dependent on the particular circumstances of the person making the estimate.
Daniel Bernouli, address to the Imperial Academy of Sciences, Petersburg (1738)

CAPITAL FULCRUM POINT

An important formula for valuing a WARRANT, which measures the minimum annual percentage increase required from the value of the underlying ordinary shares for investors to hold warrants in a company's shares in preference to the shares themselves. If, for example, the capital fulcrum point were 8% but investors expected the shares in question to rise by 10% a year until the warrant's expiry date, they would choose the warrants because these would outperform the shares. If, however, investors expected the shares to rise by only 7% then these would be a better bet than the warrants. As such, the formula is the fulcrum point above which warrants, thanks to their LEVER-AGE, become more attractive and below which ordinary shares are favoured.

The mathematical formula (see Appendix 5) works out the compound rate at which both the share price and the warrant price must grow in order for it to be equally advantageous for investors to hold either the shares or the warrants. Imagine the EXERCISE PRICE of the warrants is 100, the current share price is 145, the warrant price is 80 and the warrants expire in five years' time. By trial and error investors would eventually work out that the share price must grow by 9% a year to make it worthwhile holding the warrants to expiry. Any less than that would mean there was not enough INTRINSIC VALUE in the equation for the share price to pull the warrant price up at the same pace. Share-price growth above 9% a year would mean that the intrinsic value would swell, thus the value of the warrants – because their price is lower than the share price – would have to rise faster than the shares in order to keep the equation in balance.

Besides helping comparisons between warrants and their underlying shares, the capital fulcrum point also allows comparisons between warrants with different expiry dates because it is expressed as a DISCOUNT RATE. Take warrants in two companies which have similar prospects. If one's fulcrum point was 7% and the other's was 9% it would not matter how long each had to expiry; the likelihood is that the warrant with the 7% fulcrum point would be more attractive.

CAPITAL MARKET THEORY
The generic term for those models that aim to

price assets, usually marketable securities or portfolios of them, in terms of the trade-off between RISK and return that PORTFOLIO THEORY assumes all investors seek. The best known, and most influential, of these is the CAPITAL ASSET PRICING MODEL.

CAPITAL MARKET LINE

The graphical depiction of the trade-off between RISK and return for an EFFICIENT PORTFOLIO. In other words, it is a chart line which shows how much extra return investors would expect for taking on extra risk. Prospectively, the chart line must slope upwards (investors would not assume extra risk if they thought they were not going to get extra reward), although actual returns show that it can slope downwards for a while. This means that in the real world investors are not always rewarded for taking on higher risks. Logically this must be so; otherwise so-called higher risks would not really exist.

Arithmetically, it is calculated by taking the EQUITY RISK PREMIUM on a portfolio and dividing this by the amount of risk within the portfolio in question.

CAPITALISE

Something that companies do to costs to the benefit of immediate profits but often to the detriment of the state of the BALANCE SHEET. To capitalise is to treat a cost incurred as part of the future capital value of an ASSET. Therefore, instead of charging it against the PROFIT AND LOSS ACCOUNT, it is added to both sides of the balance sheet and written off against profits in future accounting periods.

CAPITALISATION ISSUE

See SCRIP ISSUE.

CAP-M

See CAPITAL ASSET PRICING MODEL.

CASHFLOW

Ultimately companies are processors of cash. Cash

comes in and cash goes out and companies must bring in more than they expend in order to survive. The cashflow statement, also called the funds flow statement, in a company's accounts shows how a company achieves this from year to year. In so doing, the cash statement does two other things: roughly speaking, it reconciles the income shown in the PROFIT AND LOSS ACCOUNT (income statement) with the movement of cash within the business; and, equally approximately, it reconciles the BALANCE SHEET from the start to the end of the financial year in question.

Common sense says that cashflow must be about the cash that a company brings in, from selling its goods and services and by other means, and the cash that it pays out, to suppliers, to other creditors and to providers of capital. The way that cashflow is generally shown in UK and US company accounts, however, is more about reconciling the profits or losses shown in the profit and loss account with changes in the business's underlying cash position. To do this, the cashflow statement takes net income and adds back some major non-cash charges that have been made on the income account; namely, DEPRECIATION and increases in deferred taxes. In the United States, in particular, the vagueness of the relevant accounting standard means that it is often not clear how much of a company's cashflow really is in cash.

For the investor, though, the challenge is to use the cashflow statement to get a feel for how a company is funding its dividends (since they must be paid in cash) and whether it is generating enough cash internally to fund its future growth.

A chartist must, like the oracle of Delphi, be constantly on call with predictive aphorisms, which does produce cult and cant.
"Adam Smith", *The Money Game*

CHARTIST

Someone who uses TECHNICAL ANALYSIS to forecast future prices changes of a marketable investment.

CHICAGO BOARD OF TRADE

Measured by the volume of business done in a calendar year, the Chicago Board of Trade is the world's biggest FUTURES and OPTIONS exchange. In 1999 the exchange traded 254.6m contracts, of which 191m were in FINANCIAL FUTURES. In turn, by far its biggest product in financial futures was in US TREASURY BOND futures, which accounted for 90m contracts. Its busiest year to date was 1998 when it traded 281m contracts, of which 219m were in financial futures.

The exchange was founded in 1848 and introduced futures contracts in grain in 1865. In order to meet the competition brought by electronic exchanges, it was in 2000 in the process of turning itself from a not-for-profit corporation, owned by its members, into two for-profit companies. One company, whose shares would probably continue to be tightly held by members of the exchange, would own the traditional OPEN OUTCRY method of trading that is conducted on its trading floor and that still accounts for 95% of its business. The other company would own the board's own electronic trading platform and was expected to offer its STOCK for listing on an exchange. The detailed proposals were expected to be finalised in late 2000.

CHICAGO MERCANTILE EXCHANGE

The "Merc" is the world's biggest FUTURES exchange in terms of OPEN INTEREST (the number of futures contracts outstanding at the end of any trading day). It set a world record for open interest on September 10th 1998, as cash markets crumbled, with 10.2m open positions. In 1999 its biggest day was March 11th when 8.8m contracts were outstanding. The Merc dates back to 1874 and was called the Chicago Butter and Egg Board until 1919. Traditionally, it has been stronger in agricultural products than its close rival, the CHICAGO BOARD OF TRADE, although it introduced FINANCIAL FUTURES trading in 1972 with contracts in seven currencies via its subsidiary, the International Monetary Market. The exchange is owned by its 2,725 members and is a not-for-profit corporation. However, in response to the rapid changes taking place throughout the world's major exchanges, in 2000 it declared its intention to restructure itself into a for-profit company. Similarly, it has considered abandoning its trading by OPEN OUTCRY on its 70,000 sq ft trading floor in favour of electronic trading. But for the time being, at least, open outcry trading will remain. In 1999 the Merc traded 201m futures contracts valued at $138,000 billion.

CHINESE WALL

Walls that certainly do not exist structurally and, some might suggest, not even figuratively, as they are supposed to. A Chinese wall is there to stop confidential, price-sensitive information flowing from one part of a financial institution to others where its knowledge might at best compromise or, at worst, give unfair profit opportunities to a privileged few. Most importantly, Chinese walls surround the corporate finance department of an investment bank where corporate deals are planned long before they are announced. Such information, for example, needs to be kept from the bank's fund management arm, where managers would be tempted to profit from it, and from the STOCKBROKER sales staff who might tell their own clients about it.

Chinese walls are maintained by a combination of the threat of penalties for those who are found breaking the rules and the integrity of the staff involved. Given that it is so difficult to find the source when confidential information has actually leaked out, the wonder is that Chinese walls are not breached more often.

CIRCUIT BREAKER

A stock exchange regulation to limit or postpone share trading in response to a sharp movement in the cash market or its corresponding FUTURES market. On the NEW YORK STOCK EXCHANGE circuit breakers are fine tuned every quarter with the aim of halting trading on the following basis.

- If the DOW JONES INDUSTRIAL AVERAGE falls 10% within a trading day, trading is stopped for one hour;
- If the Dow falls 20% in a trading day, trading is stopped for two hours;
- If the Dow falls 30% in a day, trading is stopped for the remainder of the day.

The specific number of points fall in the Dow needed to trigger a circuit break is set in January, April, July and October, based on the closing values of the index for the previous month. (See also TRADING COLLAR.)

CLOSED-END FUND

Known as an investment trust in the UK, a closed-end fund, like its MUTUAL FUND cousin, offers private investors the means to acquire a diversified portfolio of investments for a much smaller outlay than if they were investing directly. However, the structure of closed-end funds means they offer more than this. The "closed-end" in the title refers to the fact that closed-end funds are companies with ordinary shares that trade on a stockmarket like any other listed company. Thus the number of "units" into which a closed-end fund's portfolio is divided is fixed, unless the fund has a new share issue. For investors, therefore, putting money into a closed-end fund, or taking it out, means dealing in existing shares on a stock exchange.

Closed-end funds can, however, gain access to new capital by borrowing. In so doing, they can LEVERAGE returns for their shareholders. To do this successfully they must achieve overall investment returns greater than their cost of borrowing, otherwise the leverage works against the shareholders.

Leverage comes in a more exotic form, too: the dual-purpose fund (or split capital investment trust in the UK). In this case the fund's capital is structured to give some classes of shareholders priority over others in their claims on the portfolio's income and/or assets. Because dual-purpose funds must have a fixed life until liquidation (how else could claims on their assets be realised?) there is another effect. There is a reduction in the discount to their pro-rata portfolio value at which most closed-end fund shares trade on the stockmarket. This will not always be the case for all classes of shares in a dual-purpose fund, but it will be true for the aggregate market value of the fund's shares compared with the market value of the underlying portfolio.

Quite why so many funds trade at less than their net asset value remains a mystery. Various theories are advanced:

- that the effect of fund management charges (and sometimes the ability of fund managers) is to subtract value from the portfolio;
- that closed-end funds do not distribute all the income their portfolios generate, therefore a DIVIDEND DISCOUNT MODEL will value them at less than that of the underlying portfolio;
- that there are simply too many such funds, so laws of supply and demand dictate that for many a discount is the only price at which trades can clear. The fact that some specialist funds trade at a premium to their portfolio value gives some credence to this possibility.

COIN-FLIPPING CONTEST

An analogy that helps to justify the EFFICIENT MARKET HYPOTHESIS. Imagine that 220m citizens of the United States are all arranged into a knock-out coin-flipping contest. Each contestant who calls correctly moves to the next round; the losers are eliminated. After 25 rounds there would be just six contestants left; contestants who had done nothing exceptional except guess correctly on which side a coin was going to land. However, they might seem special because of the 220m who started they are the only ones who had called correctly 25 times running.

By the same token, those fund managers who

produce outstanding investment returns year-in, year-out may be doing nothing more than correctly guessing which shares to buy and sell. On this logic the existence of just a few investors with a record of consistent excellence does not undermine the efficient market hypothesis but is actually consistent with it, since their numbers are so few as to be in line with the numbers that chance would produce.

COMMON STOCK
US terminology for ORDINARY SHARE.

COMPOUND RETURN
The return from an investment that includes the effect of dividends or interest added to the original sum. Thus the compound rate of interest on a savings account assumes that periodically interest earned is added to the original principal and future interest is earned on both principal and interest earned. In most investment calculations compounding periods are a year (that is, the rate is expressed per year), but compounding periods can be for any length of time. The compound rate of return is the GEOMETRIC MEAN.

Compound interest –
the greatest invention of all time
Albert Einstein

CONVERTIBLE
A derivative before the term DERIVATIVES was invented. Convertibles are hybrid securities – part BOND, part ORDINARY SHARE – which are issued by companies to raise capital. They come in two forms: convertible shares (convertible bonds in the United States) and convertible preference shares (convertible PREFERRED STOCK in the United States). They breeze in and out of fashion, being favoured by the companies that issue them when interest rates are high because the OPTION to convert into ordinary shares they offer means that they carry lower interest rates than straight debt.

Investors favour them when stockmarket values look shaky because they are protected by the debt characteristics in convertibles while simultaneously retaining an exposure to shares should the market recover.

Because convertibles are essentially low-coupon bonds with embedded CALL OPTIONS, they can be valued using option valuation techniques. This is fraught with difficulties, however, particularly because the effective EXERCISE PRICE of the option changes with the market price of the convertible. In practical terms, therefore, convertibles are usually valued as EQUITY with an income advantage. Take a simplified example of a company which has convertible shares outstanding with a 6.5% COUPON and a final conversion date sufficiently far off not to be material. Assume also that the convertibles trade in the market at $80 for every $100 nominal of STOCK – which means that their DIVIDEND yield is 8.2% – and that their conversion terms are ten shares for every $100 nominal. Meanwhile, the share has a market price of $5 and its yield is 4%.

The price of the convertibles therefore comprises two components: the underlying value of the shares into which they can convert and the income advantage they offer over holding the shares. In this example, the underlying conversion value is $50; this is fairly obvious since one bond has the right to convert into ten ordinary shares which are currently valued at $5 each. The remaining $30 is the market's estimate of the extra income in today's money values that comes from holding a bond whose coupon is fixed compared with shares whose dividends will grow.

Whether that $30 is a good estimate depends on how fast dividends on the shares are expected to grow. If they manage just over 10% a year, it is a good estimate, because it will be almost eight years before the shares offer an income advantage, by which time holders of the convertibles will have accumulated about $30 of extra income at today's values.

If dividends on the shares grow faster than that,

however, less excess income will accumulate to holders of the convertibles before it is time to convert. If they grow at 15% a year, for example, only about $25 extra would accrue. In this case, the convertible would be worth only $75 ($50 of convertible value plus the income differential). Investors who expected such pacey growth in share dividends would, therefore, sell the convertible and buy the shares until the gap had been closed.

CORPORATE FILING

All well-developed securities industries demand that every company whose securities are traded on a recognised stock exchange must formally disclose relevant information about such things as: the nature and performance of the business; financial accounts; the capital structure of the company and any changes to it; material changes to the assets of the company; offers to sell new securities in the company; offers to purchase the existing securities of the company.

In the United States such information is filed with the SECURITIES AND EXCHANGE COMMISSION, which demands a whole raft of reports. The most important ones are as follows.

- 10-K. Filed annually; a comprehensive overview of the company.
- 10-Q. The quarterly financial report filed by the company.
- 8K. A report of unscheduled material events (in particular, acquisition or disposal of assets).
- 14D-1. Filed by a company making a tender offer for shares in a target company.
- 14D-9. Filed by the management of a company in receipt of a tender offer from another.
- 20-F. The annual report filed by foreign companies whose securities are listed on a US exchange.

CORPORATE GOVERNANCE

The way in which companies run themselves; in

particular, the way in which they are accountable to those who have a vested interest in their performance, especially their shareholders. Since the mid-1980s the issue has been controversial, made so by the wave of takeover activity in both the UK and the United States from that time on and by the trend for top executives effectively to pay themselves huge amounts that too often had little correlation with the performance of the business.

This situation arose because of laws that limited the power of shareholders in the United States and liquid stockmarkets that made it easier for shareholders to sell shares in problem companies rather than stay and resolve difficulties. However, the reaction is now well established with various shareholder pressure groups in both the UK and the United States urging restructured boards on to companies and demanding that top executives pay be more closely and formally linked to corporate performance. In the UK three committees, the Cadbury Committee, Greenbury Committee and Hampel Committee, have made recommendations that effectively have the force of law behind them.

"Is not commercial credit based primarily upon money or property?"
"No sir, the first thing is character."
J. Pierpont Morgan,
to the House Banking and Currency Committee, 1913

COUNTERPARTY

The party on the other side of a transaction. In the world's financial markets this means it is the party that agrees to deliver or to take delivery of a specific ASSET at a particular date and price. Counterparty RISK is a spectre that haunts the global financial system – the fear that a counterparty will fail to honour its obligations and in so doing trigger a systemic collapse where one failure leads to many. One of the big advantages of trading on a recognised stock exchange is that the exchange itself usually occupies the position of counterparty to each transaction, thus minimising this risk. OVER-THE-COUNTER markets, however, have no such fail-safe mechanism.

COUPON

The fixed periodic interest payable on a BOND, so-called because originally, and sometimes still, the security certificate had a series of counterfoils which were detached in return for the interest payment.

COVARIANCE

A key part of PORTFOLIO THEORY because it helps quantify the RISK in a portfolio; that is, the likelihood that the portfolio's returns will be less than expected. Risk is therefore determined by how volatile the returns of each of the portfolio's components are, or are likely to be. In addition, and more importantly, it is necessary to have a factor which measures the relative movements of each pair of investments within the portfolio because risk is reduced by the extent to which returns on any component in the portfolio move in opposite directions to the other components. This is the function of covariance.

The covariances of investments therefore can be as follows.

- Positive, meaning that the investments move in the same direction as each other.
- Negative, meaning that they move in opposite directions; that is, when the returns from one rise, returns from the other fall.
- Zero, meaning that the investments have no observable relation to each other.

In a theoretical world a portfolio of investments with perfect negative covariance would eliminate risk. In the real world, however, investments – certainly securities – to an extent move in the same direction. That is, there is some positive covariance. This means that risk can be reduced but not completely eliminated.

CREST

An electronic means of settling share transactions and registering investors on companies' lists of shareholders, introduced into the UK in 1996. The effect of Crest is that ownership of company STOCK is treated much like money in a bank account, with information held and transactions booked electronically. Thus share certificates, much loved by many investors but of limited use because they do not actually confer ownership of a company's shares, effectively become a thing of the past.

CUM-DIVIDEND

Stockmarket jargon which says that anyone buying particular shares is entitled to receive the next DIVIDEND that the issuer declares on those shares. Thus the market's estimate of the value of the dividend is included in the share price. (See also EX-DIVIDEND.)

CUM-RIGHTS

A share trades in the market cum-rights when the right to buy new shares in a RIGHTS ISSUE is still attached to it.

D

DATA MINING

Trawling through investment statistics, of which there are masses, to find patterns that suggest a theory, then propounding the theory. Such an approach – although widely and understandably used, given the volume of investment data and the power of today's computers – is potentially flawed because it finds the facts first then seeks to build the theory round them. Logically, it is more convincing to come up with an idea as to why something might happen and then see if the data bear it out. Some of the stockmarket anomalies which indicate that excess returns can be made by following particular trading routines are largely the product of data mining (see CALENDAR EFFECT).

DAX INDEX

See DEUTSCHE AKTIENINDEX.

DEAD CAT BOUNCE

An expression much favoured by market traders in the wake of the October crash of 1987. The analogy is between the reactions of the stockmarket and what would happen to a cat if it were dropped from the 40th floor of a tower block. On hitting the ground the cat would bounce, but it would still be dead. With such black humour did traders proffer their opinion of market rallies during that period.

DEAD CROSS

A decidedly bearish sign for a CHARTIST. It occurs when a shorter moving average for the price of a marketable investment (say, the 20-day rolling average) falls below a longer moving average (say, 50 days). The signal is much stronger if the dead cross happens after the moving averages have moved in tandem for a period, as it implies a marked change in attitude on the part of investors.

DEBENTURE

A long-term, marketable, fixed-income security issued by a company and secured against the assets of the company. In the UK a debenture is usually secured against specific assets; in the United States it is usually a floating charge on the assets in general. In either case, in the event of default on interest payments debenture holders could force the company into liquidation. If the company had issued more than one class of debenture, however, there would be a pecking order for claims on the assets.

DELTA

For speculators, one attraction of options is that they offer lots of LEVERAGE. However, the price changes of options do not follow changes in the price of the shares over which they have rights penny for penny. The price relationship between shares and their options is measured by an option's delta. This indicates the amount that the price of an OPTION will move for a given change in the price of its underlying STOCK. Say that past observations had measured the delta as 0.6. Then a 10p change in the price of the shares could be expected to produce a 6p change in the price of the option.

For a CALL OPTION the delta will always be positive, but for a PUT OPTION it will be negative. This is logical, since the price of the put will move in the opposite direction to changes in the share's price. (See HEDGE RATIO.)

DEPRECIATION

The idea behind depreciation (known as amortisation in the United States) within a company's PROFIT AND LOSS ACCOUNT (income statement) is simple and sensible enough. Its application, however, probably gives more scope for fudged figures than any other accounting item. This in turn complicates the job of assessing the value of a company's shares.

The basic idea is that the cost of a piece of capital equipment to a company should be written off over its useful life, not during the year in which the cost is incurred. This is sensible. A company's capital spending may vary considerably from one year to the next, but the flows of

D

revenue from the equipment bought should be smoother, so it is better to align the two as far as possible.

One problem arises from estimating how long the equipment will last. If the estimate is a rotten one, then implicitly the depreciation charge will be meaningless as well. Using broad-brush depreciation rates for various classes of assets solves this problem, but only partially. Then there is the effect of changes to rates of depreciation. Lengthen the economic life of an ASSET and, other things being equal, you cut the depreciation charged against the asset, thus boosting profits. Or the method of calculating depreciation may be changed from one year to the next. Most companies depreciate on a straight-line basis; that is, they write off the same sum each year. If an asset under review looks less valuable than previously thought, some form of accelerated depreciation (double declining balance, sum-of-years digits, and so on) must be used to bring the asset down to its economic value. The effect is to make an assessment of a company's true profitability more difficult. Similarly, different depreciation policies among companies in the same industry make investment comparisons trickier.

The task for an investor is to cut through these accounting obfuscations. Make sure that the depreciation provisions are conservative and apply uniform depreciation rates in comparative studies, is the sound advice of Benjamin Graham and David Dodd's SECURITY ANALYSIS.

DERIVATIVES
The generic name for financial products which are derived from other financial products and, according to some, are the ogre that threatens to bring chronic instability to the world's financial system. All derivatives contracts – whether they are OPTIONS, FUTURES, SWAPS or products with more exotic names – give one party the right (or at least the option) to make a claim on an underlying ASSET at some point in the future and bind another party to meet a counter-balancing obligation. The

underlying product might be an ORDINARY SHARE, a stockmarket index, a commodity, a string of interest payments; the list goes on.

From this, two things follow. First, derivatives can offer insurance for whomever buys contracts because they take the uncertainty out of the future value of an asset. Second, derivatives offer lots of RISK – that is, the potential to make large losses as well as large gains – for someone who does not have a cash position to HEDGE because, in return for a comparatively small payment upfront, that party accepts the consequences of what transpires in the future.

Derivatives are traded either on a recognised exchange, such as the CHICAGO MERCANTILE EXCHANGE or LIFFE, or OVER THE COUNTER (OTC), mainly by banks. In the case of the former, the exchange places itself between all market participants and therefore accepts the risks of a counterparty defaulting. In the latter case, the obligations lie with the specific parties to a contract, making OTC derivatives – implicitly at least – a greater threat to financial stability because of the panic that might ensue if, say, a major bank did default on its commitments.

> *There are two times in a man's life when he shouldn't speculate. When he can't afford it and when he can.*
> Mark Twain, *Following the Equator*

DEUTSCHE AKTIENINDEX
Simply referred to as the DAX, the leading index of German share values, comprising 30 blue-chip shares traded on the FRANKFURT STOCK EXCHANGE. It has a base value of 1,000 as at December 31st 1987, when it replaced the Borsen Zeitung Index.

DEUTSCHE BÖRSE
The company, which is owned by leading German banks, that runs the FRANKFURT STOCK EXCHANGE. The Deutsche Börse has been a driving force in attempts to consolidate European stock-

markets and in mid-2000 announced proposals to merge with the LONDON STOCK EXCHANGE to form ix, which would become the world's third biggest equities exchange, as measured by the volume of shares traded. However, plans announced in 1998 to bring the London and Frankfurt exchanges closer together stalled. Simultaneously, the Deutsche Börse announced a deal with NASDAQ to form an exchange that would specialise in trading high-technology European shares. Its own futures exchange, the DEUTSCHE TERMINBORSE, merged with the Swiss futures exchange to form EUREX in 1998.

DEUTSCHE TERMINBORSE

Germany's fast-growing DERIVATIVES exchange, which is run by the DEUTSCHE BORSE and which merged with the Swiss futures exchange, Soffex, to form EUREX in 1998.

DIRECTORS' DEALING

See INSIDER DEALING.

DISCOUNT RATE

There are two meanings.

1 The rate of interest used to express a stream of future income in today's money values. The rate used should rise as the riskiness of the income stream actually materialising grows. It is intuitively obvious that $1,000 to be received in a year's time will be less valuable than $1,000 received today. But the question arises: what exactly will it be worth? Assume a nice-and-easy discount rate of 10%; on that basis, it is also intuitive that the answer is going to be about $900. In fact it is $909, because what we really ask is: what value today will produce $1,000 in a year's time assuming a 10% interest rate? Then we work back from there and divide $1,000 by 1.1, which is the result of compounding a unit at 10% for one year.

Textbooks talk about a "discount factor" by which a future sum is multiplied to get a present value. This is simply the discount rate expressed in another way. It is the reciprocal of the compounding factor. For example, a sum compounded at 10% a year for five years will be worth 1.61 times its original value (the compounding factor). The discount factor then would be 1.61 divided by one; that is, 0.62.

2 The rate of interest at which some central banks lend money to the banking system.

DISCOUNTED CASHFLOW

Companies need benchmark tests to assess whether or not to raise funds from the capital markets for projects of their own (or whether, indeed, their own surplus funds might be better employed in capital projects or returned to shareholders). For a given level of RISK in a putative project – which, admittedly, is rather subjectively assessed – companies can find a corresponding rate of return from the markets then apply it as a DISCOUNT RATE to the likely cashflow which should be generated from the project. This analysis essentially takes two forms: an INTERNAL RATE OF RETURN calculation or NET PRESENT VALUE, which is closely related to it.

DIVIDEND

The periodic cash sum paid on a company security, be it an ORDINARY SHARE, PREFERENCE SHARE or some type of loan STOCK. Dividends on preference shares and loan stock are almost always for a fixed amount (although occasionally they are linked to an appropriate benchmark, say the rate of inflation). Dividends on ordinary shares are more variable because such shares represent the RISK capital in a business, which is entitled to residual income only after prior claims have been paid.

DIVIDEND COVER

The number of times that a company's EARNINGS per share cover its DIVIDEND per share. Investors generally regard a ratio of two or more as comfortable and anything below one and a half times as potentially risky. If the ratio sinks below one then the company is paying part of its dividend out of its retained surpluses from previous years.

This is not necessarily as bad as it sounds, because dividends are paid in cash and net surpluses in the PROFIT AND LOSS ACCOUNT are not a measure of cash. So if a company generates lots of FREE CASHFLOW it may be able to pay a dividend even though book-keeping items on the profit and loss account (for example, the need to make provisions for the falling value of assets it employs) are hitting its declared profits. However, companies can and do cut their dividends if the pay-out ratio gets too low. Conventional wisdom says that this is a matter of last resort, but research has shown that companies, particularly the smaller ones, cut dividends more often than supposed. (See DIVIDEND PAY-OUT RATIO.)

DIVIDEND DISCOUNT MODEL

A tool for valuing an ORDINARY SHARE which says that the value of the share equals the present value of all its future dividends. This is pretty uncontentious; in a sense the share's value must embrace such a flow of income, but the model also provides a basis for comparing the price of shares in the market with their theoretical value and thus judging whether the shares are cheap or expensive.

Perhaps dividend discount models suffer from being too theoretical because they are little used in the real world – especially in the UK – even though their record, such as it is, seems quite impressive. The fact that they can become quite complex and depend crucially on the quality of the estimates fed into them does not help their cause. They come in three forms.

1 Base-level model. This values shares in much the same way as bonds. Thus the assumption is that the company's DIVIDEND will remain the same forever. Consequently, the value of the shares is simply the dividend divided by the required rate of return. So if a company was expected to pay a dividend of 10p a year in perpetuity, an investor whose required rate of return was 10% would value the shares at 100p each, and one who required 12% would value them at 83p.

2 Constant growth model. This assumes that dividends will grow by the same proportion each year and, as such, is also a fairly simple calculation. It can be simplified to state that the shares' value is the next dividend divided by the required annual rate of return minus the rate at which dividends are expected to grow. If a 10p dividend is expected to grow by 5% a year, then an investor requiring a 12% return would value the shares at 150p each. The formula is:

$$10(1.05) \div (0.12 - 0.05)$$
$$= 10.5 \div 0.07$$
$$= 150$$

However, because the equation is sensitive to changes in the variables on the bottom line, someone wanting a 15% rate of return would only pay 105p (10.5 divided by 0.1).

3 Multiple growth model. This version tries to mirror reality by assuming that any company's dividends usually grow at different rates as its business moves through phases of growth, stability and decline. Take the simplest version, a two-stage model where the first stage is for a period of high dividend growth, say for five years at 20% a year, and the second for growth at a lower rate sustainable in the long term, say 10%. Assume also that the company is already paying an annual dividend of 10p and that an investor's required rate of return is 15%. A basic CASHFLOW calculation discounted at 15% tells us that the present value of the first stage's dividends is 57p.

Next apply the workings of the constant growth model to the second stage. This means grossing up the value of a 25p dividend growing at 10% by 5%. The 25p figure is the result of the 10p starting dividend growing at 20% for five years. The detail of the sum is:

$$24.9(1.1) \div (0.15 - 0.10)$$
$$= 27.4 \div 0.05$$
$$= 548$$

However, the 548p valuation arrives five years into the future. It has to be discounted to a present value at the investor's 15% required rate. This equals 272p. Therefore the overall value of the share would be 57p plus 272p, which is 329p.

DIVIDEND PAY-OUT RATIO

The DIVIDEND that a company pays expressed as a fraction of its EARNINGS. So if in a financial year a company pays a 4p dividend having declared earnings of 8p, the ratio would be 0.5. It is the inverse of DIVIDEND COVER and is generally used in the United States to define the ability of a company to fund its dividends. It is also important for its use in the adaptation of the constant growth DIVIDEND DISCOUNT MODEL to explain the PRICE/EARNINGS RATIO.

DIVIDEND YIELD

The DIVIDEND paid on a share expressed as a percentage of its market price. So if a company pays a dividend of 60 cents per share in respect of a financial year and its shares trade on a stock exchange at $25, the dividend yield would be 2.4%.

The prime purpose of a business corporation is to pay dividends to its owners.
Benjamin Graham and David Dodd, *Security Analysis*

DOLLAR COST AVERAGING

A simple and effective investment plan which virtually ensures success, as long as stockmarkets rise in the long run, as they always have done. Investors put a fixed sum into the market at regular intervals. Thus they will buy a bigger quantity of shares when the market is low than when it is high and their average buying cost will always be less than the market level while the trend remains upwards. The caveat is that in order to beat the market indexes, investors still have to select the right shares. However, nowadays regular saving plans offered by mutual funds and investment companies make dollar cost averaging simple while simultaneously spreading RISK across a portfolio of stocks.

CHARLES DOW

With Edward Jones, Charles Dow (1851–1902) founded the Dow Jones Company, which provides financial information. In 1884 he developed his first stockmarket index, an 11-STOCK index of railroad shares which went on to become the Dow Jones Transportation Average. The forerunner of the DOW JONES INDUSTRIAL AVERAGE first appeared in 1897. From 1900 until his death, Mr Dow was the editor of *The Wall Street Journal* in whose editorials he outlined what was later to be called DOW THEORY.

DOW JONES INDUSTRIAL AVERAGE

Probably the world's best-known stockmarket indicator, because of its longevity (it dates back to 1897 when CHARLES DOW produced the original 12-STOCK average) and its association with *The Wall Street Journal*, which is published by Dow Jones & Co.

The Dow is simply the arithmetical average of the prices of 30 leading US stocks and carries no weighting for the stockmarket value of its constituent companies. The effect of this is that the Dow's value is disproportionately affected by those constituents which have particularly high stock prices and, correspondingly, the influence of companies which have had stock splits declines. The inclusion of 30 of the grandest, but not necessarily most dynamic, companies in the United States means that the average is more stable than other measures of US stock values. Despite these limitations, the average is updated every minute while the NEW YORK STOCK EXCHANGE is trading and it continues to be the most widely used measure of the value of America Inc.

DOW THEORY

A theory whose original aim was to use US stock market indices to comment on the outlook for the economy. It evolved into a tool for predicting movements in the US stockmarket and reached its peak when it forecast the Wall Street Crash of 1929. Although some say it forecast the October Crash of 1987, it has since declined in importance to the extent that it has few adherents today. Nevertheless, all over the world stockmarket pundits use its concepts, usually unknowingly, to explain and predict stockmarket levels.

The theory is named after CHARLES DOW, although it probably owes more to William P. Hamilton, editor of *The Wall Street Journal* from 1908 to 1929. Essentially it says that stockmarket cycles divide into three phases.

- **Primary.** Major upward or downward movements in the market lasting usually for several years.
- **Secondary.** Movements which either reinforce the primary trend or, at defining moments, predict its demise.
- **Tertiary.** Day-to-day movements which have little significance.

The chief characteristic of a BULL market would be where both high and low points of successive secondary phases move in an upward trend, especially if this were accompanied by rising volumes of stocks traded. Thus the market would be sustained by its support levels and would break through its resistance levels. However, when the market falls through a support level and is unable to bounce beyond a previous resistance level it signals that a BEAR market has begun.

This is fine in theory, but, despite the success of the Dow theory in predicting the 1929 crash and possibly the 1987 crash, studies have shown that buying and selling a portfolio representing the DOW JONES INDUSTRIAL AVERAGE according to Mr Dow's signals would have been much less successful than a simple buy-and-hold strategy.

DOWNSIZING

The euphemism that corporate managers use for cutting out whole swathes of employees. In the UK and the United States, in particular, downsizing became a corporate imperative in the 1980s and early 1990s with, for example, the major UK telecoms operator, BT, cutting its workforce from 246,000 in 1990 to 135,000 in 1995 and IBM cutting its workforce from 407,000 to 215,000 in the eight years to 1994. The trouble is that little firm evidence exists to prove that downsizing is a successful strategy. One survey in 1994 showed that two-thirds of firms in the United States which downsized had to repeat the trick the following year. Another survey showed that the shares of corporations in the S&P 500 INDEX which downsized outperformed the index for only six months after the exercise. Thereafter they started to lag once more.

DTB

Short for DEUTSCHE TERMINBORSE.

DURATION

Several factors, such as COUPON, TERM and the prevailing level of interest rates, determine the price of a BOND. Duration is the measure that draws together all three of these into one number which quantifies the sensitivity of a bond's price to changes in interest rates. It does this in several stages. First, it puts a present value on the cashflows – the payment of dividends and principal – that will accrue to a bond over its remaining life. Second, it weights these adjusted cashflows according to what fraction of the bond's current price they comprise. Third, it multiplies each weighted cashflow by the number of years before they will be paid (a payment due in three years would be multiplied by three, and so on). Last, it adds up the totals derived from stage three.

The result – the duration – is a figure, measured in years, which says how long it will be before a bond's purchase price has been repaid in present value money. More important are the following implications:

- the higher the duration, the greater is the sensitivity of the bond price to interest rate changes;
- low coupon bonds have a longer duration, therefore they are more sensitive to interest rate changes;
- for bonds with the same coupon, the duration will be higher, and therefore the interest rate sensitivity greater, for those with a longer term to maturity;
- by modifying the calculation for duration it is possible to estimate by how much a bond's price will change for a given movement in interest rates.

EARNINGS

The proportion of a company's profits which belongs to the shareholders and, therefore, a key figure in many share valuation yardsticks. Because they are a key figure, earnings are subject to much accountancy fudging. They are generally expressed on a per share basis and are calculated by dividing a company's weighted average number of shares outstanding for an accounting period into its profits after deductions for taxation, profits belonging to outside shareholders (minorities), extraordinary items and dividends to preference shareholders. Earnings come in several formats.

- **Reported earnings.** The figure shown by the company in the regular results statements that it is required to make.
- **Underlying earnings.** The figure that is derived from reported earnings by adjusting for any one-off items that have not already been accounted for.
- **Economic earnings.** The earnings that a company could fully distribute to its shareholders without eroding the real value of capital employed in the business.
- **Fully diluted earnings.** Earnings that take account of the shares that are likely to be issued in the future, given the existence of warrants, options and CONVERTIBLE securities.

EARNINGS ANNOUNCEMENT

When companies report new earnings figures (half-yearly in the UK and quarterly in the United States), their share prices should respond rapidly to any surprise element in the figures. However, various studies have shown that there is often a sufficient time lag between the announcement and the price catch-up for some investors to make higher returns than an efficient market should permit. As such, this is an anomaly that EFFICIENT MARKET HYPOTHESIS should not allow.

EARNINGS YIELD

A useful, but largely ignored, investment ratio. At

its simplest, it is a company's EARNINGS per share expressed as a percentage of the share's market price. So if a share's earnings were 30p and the share price was 450p, then the earnings yield would be 6.7%. In other words, it is the reciprocal of the PRICE/EARNINGS RATIO (that is, $1/\text{PE} \times 100$) and has faded in comparison with that ubiquitous investment measure. Yet its value is that it describes the return on an ORDINARY SHARE in a similar way to how YIELD TO MATURITY describes the return on a BOND. It therefore helps comparisons between shares and bonds.

In the stockmarkets it is rare for the earnings yield on ordinary shares to be as much as the redemption yield on good-quality bonds. Technically, this is because the redemption value of a bond is specifically factored into its redemption yield, whereas the value of an ordinary share on disposal is implicit only in earnings yield. Additionally, and more importantly, the return on bonds is set by the terms of their issue, but the returns on shares depend on many factors, although – crucially – they are not as vulnerable to inflation as are bond returns owing to the ability of companies to reprice their products.

In comparing shares and bonds using earnings yield it should therefore be clear that shares become increasingly attractive as their yield approaches the redemption yield on bonds. Indeed, BENJAMIN GRAHAM, who is labelled the founding father of investment analysis, regularly constructed successful quantitative portfolios of shares for which he sought shares whose earnings yield was twice the yield on best-quality bonds. To put a measure of safety into such portfolios, Mr Graham also insisted that the shares of companies included had to have less debt than their NET WORTH.

EASDAQ

See EUROPEAN ASSOCIATION OF SECURITIES DEALERS AUTOMATED QUOTATION.

EBITDA

Short for Earnings Before Interest, Taxes, Depreciation and Amortisation. EBITDA is basically the cash profits that a company generates before interest and tax and is, therefore, a measure of the company's cash-generating capability. In isolation it does not mean much. However, it is useful when compared to a company's interest costs when assessing the company's potential to fund its activities through cheap loan capital rather than expensive EQUITY. For a listed company, EBITDA can be divided into its stockmarket value. The resultant ratio of market value to cash profits can then be used as a cheapness/expensiveness guide to the company's share price.

ECN

See ELECTRONIC COMMUNICATIONS NETWORK.

EFFICIENT FRONTIER

The line on a chart which marks out the best combination of RISK and return available to investors in a particular market. The theory is that all rational investors would buy assets which lie on the efficient frontier. Such assets are said to "dominate" all others, which either have less return or carry more risk. Plotting the efficient frontier therefore becomes a key aim of PORTFOLIO THEORY. In portfolio theory, as originally formalised by Harry Markovitz in the 1950s, the efficient frontier is arc-shaped because, at the margins, investors could seek extra return only by assuming disproportionate amounts of risk or sacrifice marginal returns as the price of shedding risk.

However, refinements to Markovitz's theory introduced the concept of the RISK-FREE ASSET, which investors could freely buy or borrow. The effect of putting a risk-free asset into the picture is to create portfolios whose returns cannot be bettered by standard Markovitz theory for a given amount of risk. Mathematically this must be so since the risk-free asset has a STANDARD DEVIATION of zero and therefore has no effect on the equations that shape portfolio theory. Whether investors in practice can happily buy or, more pertinently, borrow unlimited amounts of funds at the risk-free rate is another matter.

The effect was to make the efficient frontier a straight line sloping upwards, known as the CAPITAL MARKET LINE. The only point at which it touches Markovitz's arced efficient frontier – in the textbooks always picked out as point *M* for market – is where an investor would choose to put all his capital into risky market investments. All other portfolios are some combination of risky market investments plus or minus the risk-free asset. This deduction has important effects for stockmarket investors because it implies that they should do no more than buy a basket of shares that replicates the market's movements, then lever the returns up or down by combining these with borrowing or lending at the risk-free rate. As such, it is an important stepping stone towards the EFFICIENT MARKET HYPOTHESIS.

As to the point on the efficient frontier where each investor would choose to pick his portfolio, that would depend on where his own INDIFFERENCE CURVE of risk and return made a tangent with the efficient frontier. The assumption is that investors will always want better than the market offers and the point of tangent is the least unacceptable trade-off of risk and return that each investor is prepared to take.

EFFICIENT MARKET HYPOTHESIS

Arguably no investment theory has generated as much hot air as the efficient market hypothesis (EMH). This is perhaps not surprising since it is almost designed to put academics and investors into opposing camps: the academics arguing that, at its extreme, EMH renders useless all attempts to outperform the market consistently; the investors pointing to the success of various of their number in doing so. In a way there had to be an EMH. It is the natural consequence of CAPITAL MARKET THEORY, which says that excess returns for a given level of RISK are always arbitraged away, therefore returns are only what the market allows, therefore the market is efficient.

At its simplest, EMH says that security prices quickly and accurately reflect all the relevant information that might affect them. In saying this, it assumes that we are talking about stockmarkets that are sufficiently big and liquid that no single investor can influence prices and in which information moves rapidly and, in effect, at no cost. The information is made available by the army of investment analysts employed in the investment industry. However, this creates a paradox: the analysts exist only because they and their employers think that it is worthwhile to collect and disseminate information, therefore they must believe that the market is inefficient. Yet the effect of all these analysts is to make the market efficient. Which is right? Formally, EMH splits into three forms.

1 Weak. The base level form of EMH which says that security prices reflect accurately all the past price data. This might seem an irrelevance, except that it undermines the basis for TECHNICAL ANALYSIS, which assumes that past price data can give profitable clues to future price movements. Tests of weak form EMH have favoured the academics; or, at least, the failure of many studies to find patterns in security prices has put the onus on technical analysts to show that their particular methods have some validity.

2 Semi-strong. The next stage says that all published information, especially relevant financial data, is reflected in STOCK prices. This form of the theory questions the use of FUNDAMENTAL ANALYSIS: the dissection of company accounts, industry trends and so on by investment analysts. Its proof depends on various studies which examine whether excess returns can be achieved from using publicly available information. For example, do prices respond to factors such as changes in the money supply or accounting presentation? Under the latter heading, if the market is efficient share prices should respond to accounting changes which actually affect the value of a corporation, but ignore those changes which are merely presentational. The evidence is mixed. It seems that it is possible to generate excess returns from fundamental analysis, but it is extremely difficult to do so.

3 Strong. The most demanding form, which says that security prices reflect all information, both public and private. Thus even those who act on inside information cannot consistently profit by doing so. It is the easiest of the three to test for, by looking at the performance of those with the most privileged information sources: fund managers and corporate insiders. The record of fund managers undermines strong-form EMH because many studies in both the UK and the United States have shown that most retail funds – that is, mutual funds and investment companies – do not beat the market, and fewer still beat it after adjusting for the risk they bear. Studies of corporate insiders (officers or directors of companies who have to report their share dealings to the regulatory authorities) show that they are much better at producing excess returns.

The conclusion must be that large stockmarkets, such as those in New York and London, are efficient most of the time, but not always. This assessment is borne out both by the difficulty that most professional investors have in generating excess returns consistently and the familiar stockmarket anomalies which should not exist if there were complete efficiency: low P/E stock; SMALL CAP STOCK; the effect of EARNINGS announcements.

We must bring Wall Street to Main Street – and we must use the efficient, mass merchandising methods of the chain store to do it.
Charles E. Merrill, co-founder of Merrill Lynch

EFFICIENT PORTFOLIO

Within the context of PORTFOLIO THEORY, which seeks to define the trade-off between risks and returns on investments, this is a portfolio which produces the best possible return for a given level of RISK, or which offers the least risk for a given return.

ELECTRONIC COMMUNICATIONS NETWORK

The biggest threat to established stock exchanges in the near future is likely to come from electronic communications networks (ECNS), which use their expertise in data handling to allow institutional investors to buy and sell stocks more conveniently and sometimes more cheaply than on a recognised exchange, such as the NEW YORK STOCK EXCHANGE. ECNS have no function to raise new capital or to regulate listed companies, as do established exchanges. Their freedom from these responsibilities and their lack of members' vested interests mean that they can innovate more quickly than conventional exchanges. The best known ECN is probably Instinet, which is owned by Reuters, a financial information provider. In 2000 another ECN, Archipelago, announced plans to merge with a conventional exchange, the Pacific Stock Exchange, based in San Francisco.

ELLIOT WAVE THEORY

The works of a little-known accountant, Ralph Elliot (1871–1948), provide great succour to eternal optimists, because his chief idea was that stockmarkets – or, more precisely, the DOW JONES INDUSTRIAL AVERAGE, about which he wrote – basically go up. The proviso is that, according to Mr Elliot, markets go up in cycles of advance and retreat. To complicate the picture there are cycles within cycles within cycles and so on.

Mr Elliot postulated a grand supercycle, lasting 150–200 years, within which there are five supercycles within which there are five cycles within which there are five primaries. It is not too clear where these cycles begin and end, but many students of TECHNICAL ANALYSIS agree that the revival of Wall Street in 1932 was the start of a supercycle and that the BULL market which began in 1975 was the start of a cycle. Analysis of these cycles is based on waves, there being five waves which carry the market up (in which the first, third and fifth are up-waves and the second and fourth corrections), followed by three waves which take it down (the second of which is a part reversal of the

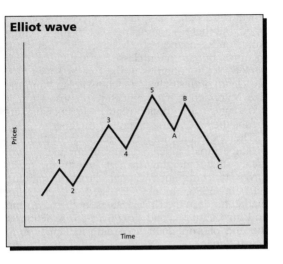

Elliot wave

Prices

Time

down trend). At the end of this eight-wave pattern the market is always higher than where it started.

Taking its cue from DOW THEORY, Elliot analysis relies heavily on patterns of support for and resistance to particular market levels. It assumes that markets are powered by the psychology of investors whose optimism grows slowly, consolidates, gets out of hand, then bursts. As such, interpretation of market charts according to Elliot principles is more art than science. However, rigidly applying the principles of FIBONACCI NUMBERS to Elliot Wave Theory can produce detailed, but contentious, estimates of the values a market should move to.

EMERGING MARKET

An emerging market is the stock exchange for a country which has a low per head income compared with the developed world and/or is not industrially developed, yet which has a functioning stock exchange, even if its standards hardly compare with those of North American and West European exchanges. There may also be stringent controls on the inward and outward flow of investment capital. As such, most of the world's stockmarkets are emerging, as opposed to developed, but there is a grey area. For example, Hong Kong and Singapore both have high per head incomes, but are often classed as emerging. Conversely, some countries in the former Soviet bloc are clearly industrialised (such as Poland and the Czech Republic), but the need to reconstruct their economies and build regulated stockmarkets means they are in the emerging category.

The potential for emerging economies to produce rapid, albeit volatile, economic growth means that emerging market investment funds have attracted much capital. From a standing start in 1986, money invested in emerging market funds in the United States, both CLOSED-END and MUTUAL FUNDS, had grown to $52.3 billion at the end of April 2000, according to Lipper Analytical Services.

EMH

See EFFICIENT MARKET HYPOTHESIS.

ENTERPRISE VALUE

A business's enterprise value is the stockmarket value of its EQUITY plus the value of the debt that it employs (some of which may also be quoted on a stock exchange). It is, therefore, a value of the total capital that the business uses. Enterprise value is used with EBITDA as a guide to the fairness of the company's valuation. Essentially, enterprise value divided by EBITDA is a ratio of business value to cash profits and can be a more useful touchstone than PRICE/EARNINGS RATIO, especially for companies that do not make much "accounting profit" (that is, profit after taking account of non-cash deductions such as AMORTISATION).

EQUITY

The high-risk capital that is committed to a business. It is high-risk because it has rights to the residual income and assets of the business only after all other claims have been met. Thus decent amounts of equity capital are crucial to a risky venture which may not make profits for some years, if at all. In contrast, low-risk businesses need comparatively small amounts of equity and can finance themselves with higher levels of debt. This has driven the trend for some cash-generating companies to increase their borrowings and return large amounts of cash to shareholders through either buying in their shares or paying out big dividends.

The major concomitant of the RISK that accompanies equity is that it brings ownership rights. In other words, owners of the equity own the business, even if for much of the time ownership is technical rather than real. (See also ORDINARY SHARE.)

EQUITY RISK PREMIUM

The extra return that investors expect from putting their capital into equities rather than a RISK-FREE ASSET; in other words, the incentive that induces them to buy ordinary shares. So it is the hope, although not the guarantee, of a reward in the future; but the difficulty, as with so much in investment, is forecasting what it might be. Historically, the existence of an equity risk premium is not in doubt. It can be measured easily, by subtracting returns on government bonds from returns on equities. The long-term premiums for the UK and United States are as follows.

Average total return (% per year)

	UK	US
Equities	17.6	16.6
Bonds	11.6	12.4
Risk premium	6.0	4.2

Within these particularly long periods, however, there have been times of sustained poor performance by equities; for example, the early 1930s and early 1970s, when there was no reward for holding equities. So investors may have good reason to doubt whether the equity risk premium will be real for their holding period.

The solution is to estimate the equity risk premium, and the simplest way to do this is to adapt the DIVIDEND DISCOUNT MODEL. Thus we can define the risk premium as the current DIVIDEND yield on equities plus the likely growth rate in dividends minus the current yield on government bonds. This will provide an answer, although it will only be as good as the estimate of growth in dividends.

EUREX
The name given to the FINANCIAL FUTURES exchange formed by the 1998 merger of Germany's DEUTSCHE TERMINBORSE and the Swiss derivatives exchange, Soffex. In 1999 Eurex signed an agreement with the CHICAGO BOARD OF TRADE to develop a joint electronic trading platform.

EUROBOND
The basic Eurobond is a FIXED-INCOME SECURITY which raises money for borrowers in a currency other than their own. It usually trades in bearer form and pays interest once a year without any deduction of tax. In addition, it accrues interest on the basis of a year comprising 12 30-day months. Most Eurobonds are listed on a recognised stock exchange – usually London or Luxembourg – although they trade OVER THE COUNTER.

Eurobond has also become a generic term for any BOND issued in the comparatively unregulated capital markets known as the EUROMARKET. As such, therefore, it includes bonds with exotic names, such as Samurai bond (technically a bond raised by a non-Japanese borrower in the Japanese market) or Bulldog bond (the same as a Samurai, but denominated in sterling and issued in the UK). The innovative nature of the Euromarket means that Eurobonds come in a variety of guises. For example:

- with warrants, which may have a variety of functions. A killer WARRANT, for example, automatically calls for redemption of its host bond when it is exercised;

- with varying interest structures from zero-coupon bonds to floating-rate bonds, whose interest payments move with money market interest rates;
- with options to redeem the bond on the initiative of either the borrower (CALL OPTION) or the investor (PUT OPTION), or no redemption at all (perpetual);
- with special repackaging. The Euromarket was largely responsible for creating the market in STRIPS. It created special securities by stripping coupons from US Treasury bonds, Australian government bonds – Dingos – and UK government gilts – Stags and Zebras.

EUROMARKET

The generic term for a vast OVER-THE-COUNTER market in promissory notes and bonds centred in London. It grew up in the 1960s through banks arranging loans in currencies held outside their country of origin. Dollars were the favoured currency because they were plentiful and internationally acceptable, and tight capital-raising regulations in the United States persuaded borrowers to look elsewhere. Big US trade deficits mean the dollar remains the core Euromarket currency, but business is now done in all major currencies.

The Euromarket was primarily developed by leading European banks, but US and, in the late 1980s, Japanese banks have since become prominent. Although characterised by a lack of regulation compared with domestic stock exchanges, the Euromarket has its own regulatory organisation, the International Securities Market Association (ISMA), and two clearing operations, Cedel and Euroclear, which work with each other. It probably raises more capital than any other market except the US domestic BOND market. The ISMA estimates that in 1999 the Euromarket's turnover was $60.5 trillion and that the value of bonds at December 31st 1999 was $2,445 billion.

EURONEXT

The name given to the planned merger of the Paris, Amsterdam and Brussels stock exchanges. If it goes ahead, Euronext will be Europe's second biggest stockmarket with a pro-forma market value of £1,494 billion for its 2,038 listed companies as at December 31st 1999. In comparison, the value of the LONDON STOCK EXCHANGE, Europe's biggest exchange, was £1,781 billion.

EUROPEAN ASSOCIATION OF SECURITIES DEALERS AUTOMATED QUOTATION

A screen-based, quote-driven market, similar to that used by NASDAQ in the United States. The European Association of Securities Dealers Automated Quotation (EASDAQ) began trading in November 1996 to give exchange trading to shares in small, fast-growing European companies which wanted to avoid the heavy, costly regulation of longer-established exchanges. In mid-2000, 58 companies were listed on EASDAQ with an aggregate market value of $56 billion. Furthermore, shares in some of the largest companies listed on NASDAQ, such as Microsoft and Cisco Systems, are traded on EASDAQ. Despite this, EASDAQ is not perceived as a great success as it faces fierce competition from the technology markets set up by established stock exchanges.

EX-ANTE

The term used to denote the fact that an investment assessment has been made with historical data (literally "from before"). Most testing of PORTFOLIO THEORY is done with ex-ante data because it is plentiful and accurate, and therefore most appropriate for testing the sometimes complex mathematics involved. There is an irony, however, because any real investment is made on an expectation of the future. In these circumstances EX-POST data ("from after") are more useful. The trouble is that ex-post data, by definition, are projected and thus less plentiful and possibly misleading. To the extent that the past often tells us something about the future, using ex-ante data is perfectly acceptable, but it does highlight a practical limitation of portfolio theory.

EX-POST
See EX-ANTE.

EX-DIVIDEND
Stockmarket jargon indicating that the price of a share is quoted minus the entitlement to a DIVIDEND which has been recently declared but not yet paid. Other things being equal, the share price will fall by the amount of the payout the day the shares are declared ex-dividend. In both the UK and the United States dividends are paid to shareholders who are registered owners (holders of record), but in order to smooth administration for a company's registrar, whose responsibility it is to distribute the dividends, stock exchanges declare a share ex-dividend a few days before the registrar closes the share transfer book. (See also CUM-DIVIDEND.)

EX-RIGHTS
When a company arranges a RIGHTS ISSUE, its existing shares trade ex-rights in the market when they no longer carry the entitlement to subscribe to their pro-rata entitlement to the new shares being issued.

EXECUTION ONLY
The no-frills, low-price share dealing service offered by a new generation of stockbrokers that has grown rapidly on the back of Internet share dealing.

EXERCISE PRICE
The price at which the right, but not the obligation, to convert an OPTION or a WARRANT into a security has been agreed. It is also known as the strike price.

FIBONACCI NUMBERS

Named after their discoverer, a medieval Italian mathematician, Fibonacci numbers almost mystically crop up in all sorts of natural phenomena, from the way petals reproduce on a flower to the shape of a galaxy. That being so, why should they not help explain patterns of stockmarket movements? Fibonacci numbers are part of a sequence in which the next number is found by adding together the previous two in the series. Thus the sequence runs 1 1 2 3 5 8 13 21 and so on.

They have a ready application in ELLIOT WAVE THEORY because Mr Elliot reckoned that each market cycle consisted of a five-wave up move followed by a three-wave down move, making eight in all. Keen devotees of the theory could then predict market tops and bottoms by using Fibonacci ratios, that is, the relationship between one Fibonacci number and its subsequent one. The most important of these are 0.6 (three

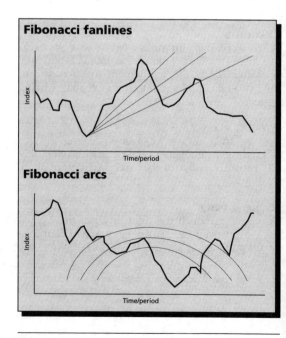

Fibonacci fanlines

Index

Time/period

Fibonacci arcs

Index

Time/period

divided by five, for example) and 1.6 (five divided by three). To give an idea of the process, in a five-wave up move, the top of wave three might be estimated by taking the market level at the top of wave one, multiplying it by 1.6, subtracting the answer from the market level at the top of wave one and adding it to the market level at the bottom of wave two. Thus if the DOW JONES INDUSTRIAL AVERAGE were 4,000 and 2,800 at the end of waves one and two, this would forecast 5,200 for the top of wave three. The sum is ([4,000 × 1.6] − 4,000) + 2,800.

In practical terms, Elliot wavers would probably use various Fibonacci ratios to calculate fan lines on a chart which would spread out from a key market bottom, thus indicating future levels of support and resistance for the market.

FIFO
See FIRST IN, FIRST OUT.

FINANCIAL FUTURES
Contracts traded on the world's FUTURES exchanges in claims of one sort or another on financial assets: currencies, interest rates, bonds or stockmarket indexes. As with futures generally, they allow risks to be hedged or big bets to be placed on future price changes. Financial futures were born in 1972 when contracts in nine currencies were introduced on the CHICAGO MERCANTILE EXCHANGE. In 1975 interest rate futures began trading on the CHICAGO BOARD OF TRADE and in 1982 the Kansas Board of Trade introduced the first stockmarket index futures contract when it began trading the VALUE LINE COMPOSITE INDEX. Since then products have proliferated. Almost all the world's major stockmarket indexes have futures contracts traded either on divisions of commodity exchanges, such as the S&P 500 INDEX on the Chicago Mercantile Exchange, or on stock exchanges, such as the NEW YORK STOCK EXCHANGE COMPOSITE INDEX, which is traded on a division of the NEW YORK STOCK EXCHANGE.

F

FIRST IN, FIRST OUT
Commonly known by its acronym FIFO, a method of accounting for stocks (inventories in US terminology) whereby the costs of the oldest stocks are deducted from revenues in computing profits. (See LAST IN, FIRST OUT.)

FIXED INCOME SECURITY
See next entry.

FIXED INTEREST SECURITY
A security on which the borrower agrees to pay regular fixed amounts of income (usually half yearly) and repay principal at a specific date. In the United States it is more generally known as a fixed income security.

FLAT YIELD
The yield on a BOND that is calculated simply by expressing its annual interest due as a percentage of its market price. So if a bond with a 10% COUPON trades at $112, its flat yield will be 8.9%. This information is of limited use since it takes no account of the fact that $12 of value will be lost over the remaining life of the bond, a factor which is, however, accounted for in the YIELD TO MATURITY (or redemption yield) calculation.

FLOATING-RATE NOTE
A type of BOND paying variable interest rates that are linked to rates in the wholesale money markets, usually the London interbank market but sometimes the market in US Treasury bills. There are variations, including the following.

- **Drop-lock bonds.** The interest rate floats until a specific event happens – usually interest rates hit a trigger point – which causes the interest rate to be fixed for the rest of the bond's life.
- **Flip-flop floating-rate notes.** A long-dated floating-rate note (FRN) can convert into a short-dated FRN and then, if the holder wishes, back into a long-dated security.

FORWARD PRICE

The price at which a transaction, probably for a currency, will be settled on a specific date in the future. Note that the term "forward" means that the ASSET being exchanged will be delivered, in contrast to the FUTURES price, where the asset will probably not be delivered but offsetting arrangements will be made.

FRANKFURT STOCK EXCHANGE

The biggest of Germany's eight regional stock exchanges whose history dates back to 1585 and which accounts for over 75% of securities trading in Germany. The Frankfurt Stock Exchange is effectively run by the DEUTSCHE BÖRSE, whose responsibility it is to ensure that the exchange's trading and settlement procedures are effective. There is computer trading of bigger stocks through its Xetra trading system as well as traditional floor trading.

FREE CASHFLOW

The cash generated by a company from its normal trading operations that is left over for the shareholders. In other words, it is the cashflow from operations less the prior claims needed to keep the business running in good order. Thus it includes deductions for capital spending as well as taxation and changes in working capital, but not dividends paid on the ordinary shares. If the information is available, it is sensible to fine-tune capital spending to exclude the cost of projects that are intended to expand the business and simply focus on replacement expenditures.

FRN

See FLOATING-RATE NOTE.

FTSE ACTUARIES ALL-SHARE INDEX

The most widely used broad indicator of London share values. Often called simply the All-Share Index, it covers 802 shares representing over 80% of the market value of shares listed in London. It dates back to 1962 and, therefore, has a long price history. It is an arithmetical index of the price of its components weighted by their stockmarket value, thus providing a more suitable base for comparing portfolio performance than an unweighted index would. Additionally, the index is broken down into ten sectors and 39 subsectors of industry, providing useful benchmarks for the share price performance of individual companies.

> *Not to bet until the odds be considered fair, reasonable or completely in the favour of the backer is an advantage which must never be surrendered. The bookmaker has to lay odds all the time for each and every race – but the backer can choose if and when to bet.*
>
> *Braddocks Complete Guide to Horse Race Selection and Betting*

FTSE 100

Now the best-known indicator of share values on the London stockmarket, even though it only started in January 1984. The index, generally referred to as the Footsie, comprises shares of 100 of the largest companies by stockmarket value listed in London. It is an arithmetic index weighted by market value, which means that the impact of price changes of the larger companies is proportionately greater than the smaller ones, thus, theoretically, mimicking the portfolios of big institutional investors. Its launch was driven by the need for London to have a suitable price index against which contracts could be written in the options and FUTURES markets. Hence its base value of 1,000, a figure sufficiently large to ensure that every day the index should move by whole numbers. Its price is continuously updated during the LONDON STOCK EXCHANGE's trading hours.

FUNDAMENTAL ANALYSIS

On the assumption that a security has a true value, which might differ from its stockmarket value, then it is the job of fundamental analysis to estimate what that true value may be. To do this, investment analysts will look at the fundamentals of the security concerned: what is likely to be the present value of the future CASHFLOW that an investor will get from the security? If it is an ORDINARY SHARE, then on what multiple of EARNINGS should it trade? In turn, this requires detailed work on the status of the issuer of the security and the economic variables that will affect it. Looked at another way, fundamental analysis is everything that TECHNICAL ANALYSIS is not.

FUTURES

Futures transfer RISK from those who do not want it to those who do. Investors with portfolios of shares who fear that the market will fall can sell their shares, but it would be a costly way of shedding risk. Alternatively, they can agree to sell a stockmarket index, say, three months in the future at its current level plus an adjustment for the interest costs they bear for carrying the portfolio. If the market falls, as expected, then the profit investors make from selling their futures contracts above the then current index level will cancel out, or at least reduce, the losses they sustain on the portfolio.

A futures contract is, therefore, a standardised forward contract. In other words, two parties agree to trade an ASSET at a point in the future. But because the trade is off-the-peg rather than bespoke, the asset being traded is precisely specified, as is the quantity traded, the settlement date for the trade and the minimum amount by which the contract price can vary. This degree of standardisation is possible because trading is conducted through a recognised exchange and comparatively few contract specifications are authorised. This has two main advantages.

1 As all trades are made with the exchange's clearing operation, the risk that the party on the other side of the transaction can default is effectively eliminated, thus generating confidence in the market.
2 Authorising only specific contracts concentrates trading in those areas, thus supplying the liquidity

– the ease of buying and selling with low TRANSACTION COSTS – on which all markets thrive.

(See FINANCIAL FUTURES.)

FUTURES OPTION

The development of markets in both options and FUTURES probably meant it was only a matter of time before the two came together. They did so in the early 1980s with the introduction of options in a range of futures in currencies, interest rates, share indices and commodities. A futures option acts much like a normal OPTION, except what is being traded is the right (but not the obligation) to be a buyer or seller of a futures contract, which is, itself, a deferred purchase or sale. As such it might seem pretty pointless, but futures options do offer scope to speculate on a futures market without being subject to margin calls if the price of the futures contract moves away from the option holder.

GAAP

See GENERALLY ACCEPTED ACCOUNTING PRINCIPLES.

GANN THEORY

As with the other main theories of TECHNICAL ANALYSIS – DOW THEORY and ELLIOT WAVE THEORY – Gann theory puts much emphasis on finding levels of support for and resistance to price changes in financial markets. However, unlike CHARLES DOW and Ralph Elliot, W.D. Gann was a successful trader in both stocks and commodities. He was also a mathematician who, like Elliot, believed that universal principles controlled the movement of markets.

The more exotic elements of Gann theory concern so-called cardinal squares. The theory's most widely used application, however, is in emphasising the relationship between price changes and time. The basic building block of this is a trend line on a chart that ascends at 45 degrees from the start price at the left-hand end of the chart. Thus the trend line plots one unit of price change for one unit of time. If actual price changes rise faster than this, the investment is in a BULL phase and vice versa. Other support/resistance lines can then be plotted on top of this showing faster/slower price changes.

GEARING

The term used in the UK to measure the proportion of debt held by a company in relation to the funds belonging to shareholders. Thus a company which had, say, total net debt of £200m and shareholders' funds of £400m would have gearing of 50% (see LEVERAGE).

GENERALLY ACCEPTED ACCOUNTING PRINCIPLES

The broad and often detailed guidelines which suggest, and sometimes dictate, how companies should draw up their accounts. The term has a special meaning in the United States because there the SECURITIES AND EXCHANGE COMMISSION (SEC) has statutory power to ensure that companies whose STOCK is traded publicly draw up their accounts according to generally accepted accounting principles (GAAP). In practice, the SEC leaves the definition of what is accepted to the Financial Accounting Standards Board, an independent body which, since its formation in 1973, has issued well over 100 accounting standards as well as a conceptual framework for accounting statements. However, occasionally the SEC has urged the standard setters to act; for example, over treatment of finance lease obligations and capitalising interest.

GEOMETRIC MEAN

In investment terms, this is the compound rate of return required to turn an initial sum into a closing sum given a specific number of compounding periods. An initial investment of $1,000 which became $2,000 after five years would have a geometric mean (compound growth rate) of almost 15% per year. Arithmetically it is defined as the nth root of the product that results from multiplying a series of numbers together where n is the number of numbers in the series.

Within investment, which devotes much attention to considering returns over particular periods of time, the geometric mean is used more often than the ARITHMETIC MEAN. However, there are occasions when using the arithmetic mean is better. Take the following series which shows year-end values and annual returns on the S&P 500 INDEX of US stocks.

	Year-end index	Return (%)
1994	459.3	…
1995	615.9	34.1
1996	740.7	20.3
1997	970.4	31.0
1998	1,229.2	26.7
1999	1,469.3	19.5

Average returns
Arithmetic mean 26.3%
Geometric mean 26.2%

If we wanted to think about the future and answer the question: what is likely to be the return from the S&P this year? Then, based on past results, the correct figure to take would be the arithmetic mean because this shows the average return in any one year. However, if we wanted to know the average growth rate that had taken the S&P from 459.3 to 1,469.3 over the five years from end-1994 to end-1999 then the geometric mean would be the one.

Note that unless the numbers in the series all change by the same rate, the geometric mean will always be less than the arithmetic mean; and the difference between the arithmetic and geometric means will widen as the variability of the series increases.

GILT-EDGED STOCK

Or simply gilts. The name for bonds issued by the UK government to fund its debt; so-called because the likelihood of default on either interest payments or principal was (and is) effectively zero. As at March 1999 there were £292 billion of gilts outstanding, which comprised 77% of the UK government's debt. Of these stocks, £62 billion was in INDEX-LINKED GILTS and almost all of the remainder in conventional fixed-interest stocks.

GLASS-STEAGALL ACT

A 1933 act of the US Congress which separated commercial banking – that is, taking deposits and lending on the funds at a margin – from INVESTMENT BANKING – that is, underwriting securities issues and investing in equities. The effect was to split up the banking empire of J.P. Morgan into Morgan Guaranty Trust and Morgan Stanley, and the act continues to restrict the ability of commercial banks to diversify into investment banking in the United States. Even though it is fraying at the edges and there have been attempts to repeal it for many years, it remains in force.

GOLDEN CROSS

Moving averages move technical analysts and

rarely more so than when they form a golden cross on a price chart, or its bearish opposite, a DEAD CROSS. A golden cross is where a short moving average (say, the rolling average of 20 days) breaks above a longer moving average (say, 50 days). The signal will be so much the stronger if the cross is formed after the moving averages have stayed close to each other for some time, since this indicates a shift in the market's perception of the STOCK in question and a willingness to take it to new higher ground.

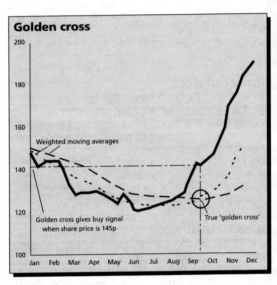

Golden cross

Weighted moving averages

Golden cross gives buy signal when share price is 145p

True 'golden cross'

Jan Feb Mar Apr May Jun Jul Aug Sep Oct Nov Dec

GOODWILL
That indefinable something that makes a business special. Because it is indefinable it cannot be separated from the rest of the company's assets and therefore cannot be included in its BALANCE SHEET as part of its NET WORTH. However, it can be included if it is goodwill which has been acquired when buying another business. If it is included in the balance sheet of a US corporation it has to be depreciated against revenues over a maximum of 25 years. In the UK, where the rules were changed

G

in 1998, a 20-year write-off period is the norm. In the past, UK companies generally wrote off acquired goodwill against their capital reserves.

The effects of including or excluding goodwill from balance sheets is the same as including or excluding INTANGIBLE ASSETS, and the debate about the merits of doing either generates the same amount of hot air. For investors who want to assess the value of a business, the sensible course is generally to include acquired goodwill in the balance sheet as this gives a better idea of how much capital has been used to generate its profits.

BENJAMIN GRAHAM

Often referred to as the "Dean of Security Analysts", Benjamin Graham (1894–1976) more than anyone gave formal structure to the process of investment analysis. He did this by rigorous analysis of the financial statements of corporations as detailed in SECURITY ANALYSIS, which he co-wrote with David Dodd and which, over 60 years after publication, remains an important text. His more accessible book, *The Intelligent Investor*, deals more with the psychology of investing and has been in print continuously since it was published in 1949. Mr Graham was a successful investor in his own right and funds managed by his business, Graham-Newman Corporation, grew by 21% a year between 1936 and 1957. His teachings are synonymous with VALUE INVESTING and he is, perhaps, best known as the mentor of WARREN BUFFETT.

The different systems – Ben Graham, growth stocks – are fine, as long as you have the discipline to stick to them... Myself, I have no system. I'm a pragmatist. I just wait until the fourth year, when the business cycle bottoms, and buy whatever is offered.
Larry Tisch, from *The Money Masters*

GREENMAIL

A form of blackmail practised by one company on another, primarily in the United States where the rough and tumble of takeover bids is more aggressive than in Europe.

One company builds up a substantial shareholding in another, then threatens either to mount a full-scale bid or to sell its stake to another potential bidder unless the management of the company under threat agrees to buy out the shareholder for a substantial profit. Managements counter the threat of greenmail by putting in place POISON PILL plans.

GREY MARKET

The trading that takes place between the launch of a new share issue and the delivery of allotment letters, which tell applicants how many shares they have received. Such trading is, therefore, done at RISK because sellers do not know how many shares they have and buyers may not know the price at which the shares have been allotted. This does not stop sometimes active grey markets developing, especially in shares of utilities privatised by the UK government. In these, grey markets have been encouraged by the LONDON STOCK EXCHANGE, as it begins its official dealings before allotment letters have been delivered.

HANG SENG INDEX

The main stockmarket index for Hong Kong. It comprises shares in 33 blue-chip companies and is computed as the ARITHMETIC MEAN of their price changes weighted by their market capitalisations.

HEAD AND SHOULDERS

Among the patterns that technical analysts search their charts for, head and shoulders patterns are among the best known and, with hindsight, can be applied to some of the great stockmarket crashes of history, from the SOUTH SEA BUBBLE of 1720 to the October crash of 1987. The idea is that following a sustained run-up in the price of a STOCK (or a market) the price reaches a new high based on heavy volume of trading then subsides (the left shoulder). This is followed by another surge to a new high, but probably based on lighter volume (the head). Following another correction the price surges again but on much lighter volume and fails to reach its previous high (the right shoulder). If the price then falls below the neckline – that is, the line which underpins the previous lows formed in both shoulders – this would be taken as a strong sell signal.

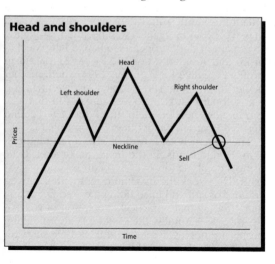

Head and shoulders

HEDGE

To hedge is to remove RISK from a transaction that will take place some time in the future. Thus, in the standard explanation, a commodity producer will agree to sell its goods at a specific price on a specific date in the future, and a commodity processor will agree to buy them. The two parties have nullified the risks they each faced: the producer the possibility of having to sell in a falling market; and the processor the risk of having to buy in a rising market.

The idea carries over into the financial markets. The equivalent of the commodity producer is an investor with a portfolio. The investor is LONG of stocks and in selling an appropriate number of contracts in the FUTURES of a STOCK index effectively protects the value of his portfolio against an overall fall in the value of stocks. The equivalent of the commodity processor is someone who is prepared to go long of stocks some time in the future, probably a SPECULATOR or an investor who needs to unwind an earlier hedge.

HEDGE FUND

An investment vehicle best known for its excesses: excessive profits, as in 1992 when the Quantum Fund, run by GEORGE SOROS, took a massive position against sterling, then struggling to remain in the European Exchange Rate Mechanism, and reputedly pocketed over $1 billion in profit; excessive losses, as in 1998 when another hedge fund, Long Term Capital Management, on whose board sat two Nobel Laureates in financial economics, needed help from the US Federal Reserve Board to bail it out of billion-dollar losses.

These snapshots, however, give a false impression. Hedge funds, in the main, HEDGE their bets, using a combination of cash securities and DERIVATIVES. They seek the maximum returns for a given amount of RISK and in so doing are – so far, at any rate – the ultimate practical expression of PORTFOLIO THEORY. Naturally, their attempts at arbitraging profits are not always successful, as 1998 showed, and in 2000 Mr Soros's hedge fund lost heavily as it was exposed to rapidly falling share prices among technology stocks. Yet the track record of hedge funds probably leaves conventional funds behind. Only "probably" because information on their collective performance is sketchy. In mid-1998 it was estimated that $300 billion worldwide was managed in hedge funds, most of it coming from wealthy individuals. One estimate puts their annual compound returns since 1988–98 at over 18%, compared with 7.5% for the Morgan Stanley Capital International World Index.

HEDGE RATIO

Options can insure a portfolio of shares as well as being speculative, and the hedge ratio, which predicts how much an OPTION's price will move for a given change in the price of the underlying shares, defines how much exposure to options is likely to be needed to hedge a position in ordinary shares perfectly. The ratio is derived from the BLACK-SCHOLES OPTION PRICING MODEL and holds good to the extent that the future VOLATILITY of the share price echoes its past.

Assume, for example, that an investor has a holding of 5,000 shares in a company, that the standard US arrangement of 100 shares per options contract applies and that a hedge ratio for call options in the shares is 0.6. To hedge his position fully the investor will need to write (that is, sell) 83 call options: 5,000 ÷ (0.6 × 100).

HORIZON PREMIUM

The excess return that investors seek for holding comparatively risky long-term bonds as opposed to comparatively safe short-term bonds, or Treasury bills. Over the long term in the United States this premium has been about 1.5 percentage points, although interestingly it has been rather less in the UK, where inflation (and therefore short-term interest rates) has been consistently higher. It can, therefore, be used as a cheapness or expensiveness indicator for long-term bonds.

IMMUNISATION

The investment strategy for protecting a BOND portfolio against the risk of rising interest rates. Theoretically, this is possible because of the twin effects of rising rates. They depress the price of bonds, but they raise yields, therefore allowing future income to be reinvested at higher rates than previously expected. A bond portfolio would be immunised if its DURATION equalled the investor's expected investment period. However, this is more theoretical than real because the portfolio would have to be continually rebalanced so that its duration matched the investment period.

IN THE MONEY

Assume we are dealing with a CALL OPTION, which gives the holder the right to buy a share, then the OPTION contract will be in the money if the market price of the underlying shares is greater than the price at which the option holder can exercise his rights. Say a share trades at 430p, then an option to buy that share at 400p will be 30p in the money. Another way of putting this is that it has 30p of INTRINSIC VALUE because anyone would pay at least 30p to acquire this option.

Note that for put options the opposite is the case. A PUT OPTION is in the money when the market price of the share is less than the price at which the option holder can sell the share.

INCOME STATEMENT

See PROFIT AND LOSS ACCOUNT.

INDEX ARBITRAGE

A particular type of PROGRAM TRADING which, according to some, was largely responsible for the spectacular fall in share values on Wall Street in October 1987.

Index arbitrage essentially works by taking advantage of any anomalies that occur between the value of a basket of stocks which can replicate a STOCK index – say the S&P 500 INDEX – and the value of an options or FUTURES contract in that index. If the basket of stocks is expensive compared with the index futures, traders will sell the stocks and buy the futures, or vice versa, until any worthwhile profits opportunity has been priced away. This is easier said than done because the basket of stocks has to be bought or sold quickly and this requires sharp organisation.

The trouble most often arises on the day when the options or futures contracts expire. This causes the value of the contracts and the value of the stocks used as a substitute for the index to align, as they must (otherwise there would be no profits for those who have successfully hedged). This can cause massive trading, buying or selling, in the underlying securities and consequently rapid movements in the market indexes.

Investors should understand that what is good for the croupier is not good for the customer. A hyperactive stockmarket is the pickpocket of enterprise.
Warren Buffett, chairman, Berkshire Hathaway

INDEX FUND

The inability of most professional fund managers consistently to beat the returns on major stock-markets led to the growth of index funds. Known as tracker funds in the UK, they are portfolios constructed so that their returns mirror as closely as possible those of a chosen index, most commonly the S&P 500 INDEX in the United States and the ALL-SHARE INDEX in the UK. This is achieved by either holding every share in an index in line with its market-value weighting within the index or, more likely, holding a basket of shares whose aggregate returns have matched the index in the recent past and so, the assumption goes, are likely to do so in the future. By adopting this low-key approach such funds expect to save on running costs which, in itself, will be an important factor in ensuring that returns match the index more closely. Thus, predictably, a MUTUAL FUND that aims to track an index will include low charges as part of its marketing pitch.

INDEX-LINKED GILTS

UK government securities whose principal and interest payments are tied to the Retail Prices Index (RPI), the most widely used measure of inflation in the UK. Index-linked gilts were first issued in 1981 in response to widespread demand from investing institutions during a period of sustained high inflation in the UK. In theory, they allow institutions with long-term liabilities, which can be closely defined, to match their assets to those liabilities. They have never been especially popular, however, perhaps because their returns have rarely compared with those consistently generated by risky equities.

Moreover, the index-linking they offer is selective. First, because the RPI may be an inadequate benchmark for some investors (pension funds, for example, may prefer to link their liabilities to the rise in wages, not prices). Second, an index-linked gilt is not actually linked to the change in inflation during its life. Rather, it is tied to the level of RPI eight months before it was issued until eight months before it is redeemed. The need to be able to calculate the value of both dividends and redemption within a reasonable time made such an adjustment almost inevitable. However, it does mean that investors holding an index-linked gilt to maturity face some residual RISK, which may work for them or against them.

INDEX-LINKED SECURITY

Any security whose redemption value and dividends are tied to an index, most probably the changes in a relevant stock exchange index or the security's domestic rate of inflation. Best known are INDEX-LINKED GILTS, although in the UK several investment trusts have issued stocks which are tied to a stockmarket index. In the 1970s the French government issued a BOND which was linked to the price of gold. From the borrower's point of view it was a disaster.

INDEX OPTION

By far the most popular form of OPTION, the index

option allows investors to speculate on movements in stock exchange indices or to insure their portfolios against unfavourable changes in STOCK values. Index options for most major indices are available nowadays. For example, the S&P 500, the NEW YORK STOCK EXCHANGE COMPOSITE INDEX, the NASDAQ 100 Index and others on various US exchanges (although the Chicago Board Options Exchange dominates); the FTSE 100 Index in London; the CAC 40 INDEX in Paris; and the DAX INDEX in Frankfurt.

The major difference between index options and stock options is that settlement is always for cash, whereas stock can be delivered as settlement with stock options. Effectively, therefore, traders in index options pay and receive a unit price per point of the underlying index; $100 per point on the S&P 500 INDEX, for example, and £10 per point on the FTSE 100. So if, say, the New York Stock Exchange Composite Index closed at 505, then someone with a CALL OPTION on the index with a STRIKE PRICE of 500 could exercise the option and make a gross profit of five times $100.

In addition, note that options on the S&P 500 are European-style options which do not allow early exercise. In London's LIFFE market investors get a choice between European-style and American-style options on the FTSE 100; options on the CAC 40 are American-style.

INDIFFERENCE CURVE

A concept from the theory of consumer demand which has an application in PORTFOLIO THEORY. On a chart the curve shows all the combinations of two things to which a consumer is indifferent; that is, the consumer will accept the combination of the two offered at any point on the curve. In portfolio theory the two variables are risk and return. So the curve illustrates the degree of risk that an investor will assume for a given reward, and vice versa. When juxtaposed with the risk or reward trade-off that a market actually offers, the point at which the investor's indifference curve makes a tangent with the line of the market risk or return (known as the EFFICIENT FRONTIER) is where the investor would choose his portfolio.

INDIVIDUAL RETIREMENT ACCOUNT

A US tax shelter for income that is being saved for retirement. Single people can shelter $2,000 annually and married couples $4,000. Individual retirement account (IRA) contributions are tax deductible for people with annual income below $25,000 and partially deductible for incomes of $25,000–34,999 for singles and $49,999 for marrieds. Eligible investments are a wide range of stocks, bonds and managed funds. All income that accrues is tax free until withdrawal.

INDIVIDUAL SAVINGS ACCOUNT

The UK government's tax-free savings vehicle that replaced the PERSONAL EQUITY PLAN and the TAX-EXEMPT SPECIAL SAVINGS ACCOUNT in April 1999. In each of the two financial years following the introduction of individual savings accounts (ISAS), individuals have been able to put up to £7,000 into an ISA in a wide range of investments that include shares in EU companies, unit trusts, investment trusts and, to a limited extent, savings accounts and life insurance products. In the tax year 2001/02 and beyond, the maximum will fall to £5,000.

INITIAL PUBLIC OFFERING

When shares in a company are offered to outside investors for the first time and simultaneously the company arranges to have its shares listed for trading on a recognised stock exchange. Usually, though not necessarily, in an initial public offering (IPO) the company raises new capital for its own uses and some of the existing shareholders sell some of their holdings.

INSIDER DEALING

There are two distinct and different meanings.

1 Illegal dealings in securities (most often purchases) by people with confidential information which they use for their own gain or that of associates. The archetypal case is of someone in the corporate finance department of a STOCKBROKER or an investment bank who knows that a company will shortly be in receipt of a bid from another and buys shares in the target company to profit from any jump in the share price that follows the announcement of the bid. Practices such as this are illegal in all major financial centres, although they remain notoriously difficult to prove and convictions are few and far between.

2 The purchase or sale of shares in a company by its directors during periods when it is perfectly proper for them to deal. The practice is watched closely on the basis that a company's directors know more about it than any outside observers and therefore their actions are a good guide to its prospects. Directors' sales may not be so important. They may sell shares for any number of reasons. However, purchases by clusters of directors where they put a significant amount of new money into their shares (that is, the shares are not purchased solely through the exercise of options awarded as part of their remuneration packages) can often be a useful indicator of good things in store for a company. In the UK it is more often known as "directors' dealings".

> *Avoid "inside information"*
> *as you would the plague.*
> Philip L Carret, from *The Art of Speculation* (1930)

INTANGIBLE ASSETS

The process of valuing and deciding whether to include or exclude intangible assets from a company's BALANCE SHEET is a wonderfully grey area for accountants and therefore a source of confusion for investors. Basically, intangibles are assets without a physical form (they are not plant and equipment), which are separately identifiable from a company's other assets and to which a stream of revenue can be attributed. Patents, copyrights and franchises are archetypal intangibles. More controversially, in the UK brand names which have been acquired are also intangibles, but brands which have been built up are rarely classified as such.

Classification of what comprises intangible assets and how they are accounted for matters because it affects both the NET WORTH of a company and its EARNINGS. Including intangibles on the face of the balance sheet increases the net worth, but their value generally has to be depreciated (always in the United States) and this reduces earnings. Excluding them – that is, writing off their value against the capital reserves of the business – is good for earnings but not for net worth. The debate continues. (See also GOODWILL.)

INTERNAL RATE OF RETURN

The DISCOUNT RATE which, when applied to a series of cashflows, would make their value net out at zero when expressed in today's money values; that is, the present value of the cash received from an investment would be the same as the present value of acquiring that cash. As such, the internal rate of return (IRR) is used to test investment opportunities against a benchmark rate of return. If the IRR on an opportunity is likely to be higher than the benchmark, the investment is viable; if not, forget it.

The IRR cannot be solved directly but has to be found by trial and error. If an investment's cashflows produced a value of –$2,000 over its life when a 15% discount rate was used and a value of $10,000 with a 10% discount rate, then common sense says that the IRR will be nearer to 15% than 10%. This is simply because –$2,000 is closer to zero than $10,000. How much closer is defined by the difference between the discount rates chosen and the gap between the valuations they produce. In this case the difference between discount rates is 5 percentage points and the gap between the values they generate is $12,000, that is, $10,000 – (–$2,000). Thus the IRR will be ten-twelfths of the gap between 10% and 15%. The sum is:

$$\text{IRR} = 10\% + [(10 \div 12) \times 5\%] = 14.2\%$$

Doing a calculation such as this long-hand is time consuming. Happily, however, financial calculators and computer spreadsheets invariably have the ability to do the iterative process quickly and accurately. (See YIELD TO MATURITY.)

> *I've worked myself up from nothing*
> *to a state of extreme poverty.*
> Groucho Marx

INTRINSIC VALUE

An expression that has a specific meaning and ones of increasing vagueness.

- The specific definition applies to options and warrants in which the intrinsic value is what an investor must pay for the right to buy or sell a share at some point in the future. So if the price of a share were 150p and there was an OPTION to buy it at 120p, someone must be prepared to pay 30p for that privilege. Thus the intrinsic value is defined as the share price minus the EXERCISE PRICE, assuming the result is positive.

- More vague, the intrinsic value of an investment is all the cash that it will ever generate expressed in current monetary values. In a sense this must be so; all it is saying is that a share is worth no more than it is worth. The difficulty lies in finding what that value is. In investment analysis, for example, the intrinsic value of a company is often defined as all the future FREE CASHFLOW discounted to present value. This is fine in theory, but forecasting all those cashflows is impossible and the correcting mechanism of adding a RISK premium into the chosen DISCOUNT RATE to allow for all those unknown factors falters because of its subjectivity.

- So vague as to be useless, sometimes it is argued that some objects, usually gold, have intrinsic value regardless of their market price. This claim is most likely to be trotted out by people with a vested, not to say desperate, interest in seeing the market price move in their favour.

INVESTMENT BANKING

This is a bit of a misnomer. It is the type of banking associated with firms such as Morgan Stanley, Goldman Sachs and Credit Suisse First Boston and which, arguably, is not banking at all. Its roots lie in the separation of deposit-taking banking from banking involving the underwriting of securities offerings. This division was forced in the United States by the 1933 GLASS-STEAGALL ACT, which was passed in response to the speculative excesses of some banks in the 1920s, which were exposed by the 1929 stockmarket crash.

Nowadays investment banking is synonymous with the financial conglomerates which conduct a full range of investment-related activities from advising clients on securities issues, acquisitions and disposals of businesses, arranging and underwriting new securities issues, distributing the securities and running a fund management arm. The growing presence in investment banking of European and Japanese banks not limited by Glass-Steagall, and the ability of some US commercial banks to circumscribe the act, mean that the division between investment and commercial banking is increasingly artificial.

INVESTMENT TRUST

See CLOSED-END FUND.

IPO

See INITIAL PUBLIC OFFERING.

IRA

See INDIVIDUAL RETIREMENT ACCOUNT.

IRR

See INTERNAL RATE OF RETURN.

ISA

See INDIVIDUAL SAVINGS ACCOUNT.

iX

The name for the stock exchange that will result from the proposed merger between the DEUTSCHE BORSE and the LONDON STOCK EXCHANGE. iX is an abbreviation for international exchanges.

JANUARY EFFECT

January is different from other months in the stockmarket. A study of market returns in 16 countries found that in 15 of them January produced above-average returns and that this effect is strongest in the UK and the United States. For example, a study of US STOCK returns for 1904–74 showed that the average monthly return was 0.5%, but for January it was 3.5%. Furthermore, in the United States the feature is concentrated on the stock of small corporations. The DOW JONES INDUSTRIAL AVERAGE of 30 leading corporations showed no January effect. This could be for tax reasons, because stocks are sold towards the end of the tax year in December, then bought back at the start of the new tax year. As the UK's tax year runs till the end of March this does not explain why the UK has a January effect; indeed, for small British companies January is the worst month of the year. The fact that stocks which pay no dividends or those with a high yield also do well supports the notion that January's excess returns are essentially a catch-up exercise. The odd thing is that this phenomenon persists even though it is so well known.

JAPANESE CANDLESTICK CHART

So called because each entry looks like a candlestick and the charts originated in 19th century Japan, where they were used to follow the rice market. These charts are a sophisticated version of charts which show the high, low and closing price of a marketable investment. The fact that they come from the mysterious east and have exotic names to describe some of their formations – hanging man, dark cloud cover, *doji* – adds to their attraction. More importantly, they pack a lot of information into a small space.

JUNK BOND

A type of security that took corporate America by storm in the 1980s. Strictly speaking, junk bonds are fixed-income securities that fail to make investment grade; for example, they are below grade BB according to Standard & Poor's BOND RATING.

Japanese candlestick chart

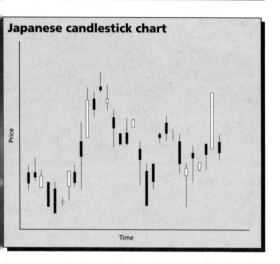

Many of them became junk bonds by being "fallen angels"; they started out as investment grade, but fell. However, in the 1980s an OVER-THE-COUNTER market in junk bonds was underwritten primarily by STOCKBROKER Drexel Burnham Lambert specifically to fund corporate deals (mergers, takeovers, restructurings). The justification for this was that junk bonds were far less risky than was thought and therefore the excess yields they offered easily compensated investors for the extra RISK involved in holding them. Their success was phenomenal. The par value of junk bonds outstanding rose from $15 billion in 1980 to over $200 billion in 1989.

Debt isn't good and it isn't bad.
Michael Milken

However, default rates rose too, reaching 9% of the par value of bonds outstanding in 1991. That was the year that Michael Milken, the driving force behind Drexel's domination of the junk market, entered prison for a ten-year sentence (subsequently reduced) after pleading guilty to charges of felony, bribery and racketeering relating to junk securities. Drexel had filed for bankruptcy the year before.

KEOGH PLAN

A US tax shelter for self-employed people saving for their retirement. Each year someone who is self-employed can put 20% of their income up to a maximum $30,000 into a Keogh plan. Contributions are tax deductible, although proceeds cannot be withdrawn without penal tax rates until the plan member is 59½ or becomes disabled. Common stocks, bonds and mutual funds are all eligible for inclusion in the plan and the income accrues tax free until it is withdrawn.

KONDRATIEF CYCLE

A long-term cycle in economic activity identified by a Russian economist, Nikolai Kondratief. By studying the economies of the UK, the United States and France, Mr Kondratief suggested cycles of 48–54 years' duration which were driven by long-term demands for capital and sustained, for a while anyway, by the rising wealth that the capital investment created. Subsequent work on his ideas suggests that his cycles peaked in 1812, 1866, 1920 and 1974.

LAST IN, FIRST OUT

How a company accounts for its stocks (inventory in US terminology) has a big effect on the profits it declares and the taxes it pays. The United States is unusual because its tax authorities are among the few that allow companies to account for their STOCK on the basis of last in, first out (LIFO). This means that the stock whose cost is first of all deducted from revenues for computing profits is that which was most recently purchased. Assuming that the cost of stock rises, then the effect is to minimise both declared profits and tax payable. It is logical in so far as it excludes profits which are simply the result of the fortuitous gain in the value of stock and it shows profits in a conservative light. In those industries where the cost of raw materials often falls (notably some branches of the electronics industry) it is equally logical to apply FIFO costings to stock, and this does happen. The aim for investors, however, is to establish which method of stock calculation a company is using – by no means easy given the variations available – and adjust for consistency with comparator companies. Analysts of US corporations are helped by reporting regulations that require corporations using LIFO accounting to show comparable FIFO figures.

LEVERAGE

One of the wonders of capitalism, but always a potential horror, too: the means by which investment returns are enhanced through using fixed costs which have first call on a stream of income or a fund of capital. Leverage (better known as GEARING in the UK) pervades all investment-related areas.

Operational. By their nature all companies use leverage in their everyday operations because many of their costs are fixed or, at least, sticky (that is, they rise with extra business activity, but not much). Thus marginal income becomes particularly valuable because a high proportion of it feeds straight through to profits.

Financial. Companies add to their leverage through their financial structure because, for the most part, the cost of debt and preference shares is fixed. Thus once the obligations on these have been covered, extra revenues belong either to the ordinary shareholders or to the tax man. It is within the context of companies' financial structure that the term is most often used. Hence highly leveraged buy-out, a practice common since the mid-1980s where a business's managers substitute much of the firm's EQUITY with debt in order to enhance returns on the shares of which they are likely to be substantial holders.

Investment. Like a company's, investors' returns can be improved by borrowing. Clearly, if the cost of debt is, say, 12% a year and investment returns are 15%, then all the excess returns on that portion of a portfolio funded by debt belong to the investors, raising the average return on their own capital. Some canny investors even manage to borrow money without cost. For example, insurance companies have the free use of a pool of money paid to them by policyholders, which they can invest until it is needed to meet claims.

Exotic leverage. Some companies have complicated capital structures in which several layers of shareholders have rights to income or capital, with each successive group in the pecking order having a more leveraged exposure to remaining funds. These are usually closed-end funds where, for example, the first call on distributable income may go to preference shareholders. First call on capital may belong to zero-coupon preference shares whose return depends on getting a lump sum when the company is liquidated. Remaining income and capital might then go to ordinary shareholders, whose investment would necessarily be a risky one.

LIFFE

See LONDON INTERNATIONAL FINANCIAL FUTURES AND OPTIONS EXCHANGE.

LIFO

See LAST IN, FIRST OUT.

JESSE LIVERMORE

One of the great speculators in US stocks in the first third of the century, Jesse Livermore (1887–1949) made his greatest killing when he sold STOCK SHORT ahead of the Wall Street Crash of 1929. By 1931 his fortune was estimated at $31m, but by 1934 he had lost it all and filed for bankruptcy, his life ruined by the discovery that his alcoholic wife was having an affair with a prohibition agent. In 1949 he killed himself in the men's room in New York's Sherry-Netherland Hotel. Nowadays he is best remembered via the fictionalised account of the early part of his career in Edwin Lefevre's *Reminiscences of a Stock Operator*, which, over 70 years after its publication, remains in print and widely read.

> *Tips! How people want tips!*
> *They crave not only to get them, but to give them.*
> *There is greed and there is vanity.*
> Edwin Lefevre, *Reminiscences of a Stock Operator*

LONDON INTERNATIONAL FINANCIAL FUTURES AND OPTIONS EXCHANGE

As measured by the value of contracts traded, the London International Financial Futures and Options Exchange (LIFFE) remains Europe's biggest FINANCIAL FUTURES market and the world's second largest behind the CHICAGO MERCANTILE EXCHANGE. In 1999 LIFFE traded 118m contracts with a nominal value of £50.4bn. That said, the late 1990s were traumatic times for the exchange as it lost business in its major product – German bund futures – to EUREX; in 1997, before its crisis, LIFFE traded 209m contracts. As a consequence of its problems, LIFFE abandoned both its system of trading by OPEN OUTCRY in favour of a screen-based system and its mutual ownership whereby it was owned by its members. LIFFE's major product now is in a benchmark interest rate futures product for the euro, Euribor, which in 1999 accounted for 45% of the value of business done on the exchange. LIFFE opened for trading in 1982 and merged with the London Traded Options Market in 1992 and with the London Commodity Exchange in 1996, which extended its trading range into soft commodity futures, such as cocoa, coffee and sugar.

LONDON STOCK EXCHANGE

In recent years the London Stock Exchange has looked like an organisation struggling to cope with the pace of change in the world's stockmarkets. Despite this, it remains the world's fourth largest stockmarket measured by the market value of its listed companies and is by far the biggest exchange in Europe. At the end of 1999 the aggregate value of the 2,292 companies whose shares were listed on the London exchange was £1,781 billion. In comparison, the market value of companies listed on the NEW YORK STOCK EXCHANGE, the world's biggest exchange, was £6,932 billion; and the value of the PARIS BOURSE, Europe's second biggest equity market, was £893 billion.

However, in 2000 the exchange announced its intention to merge with Frankfurt's DEUTSCHE BORSE to form a new exchange to be called ix, which will trade all the stocks and DERIVATIVES traded on both the London and Frankfurt exchanges. Regulation of the stocks listed will be based on London's model and the trading system will be based on Deutsche Börse's model. This move is in response to institutional investors' demands that share trading be made cheaper. If it goes ahead, it will end the London Stock Exchange's 230 years of independence, which began in 1773 when London stock brokers and stock jobbers (wholesalers) moved out of Jonathan's coffee house into their own premises.

Henry, why do people who have enough money try to get more money?
Ruth Wilcox to Henry Wilcox in E.M. Forster's *Howards End*

LONG

A term generally applied to those taking speculative positions in a market, or those whose job it is to supply a market with liquidity (market makers in London, specialists in New York). Thus if traders are long of STOCK they hold the stock in question and consequently may be vulnerable to sellers appearing in numbers (see SHORT).

LOW PRICE/EARNINGS RATIO STOCK

One of the stockmarket anomalies that seems to produce consistently high returns: that investing in a portfolio of diversified stocks which have a low PRICE/EARNINGS RATIO (P/E ratio) will generate better returns than the market average or a similar portfolio of high P/E ratio stocks. Evidence for this has been found in many studies in both the UK and the United States. The excess returns may have been concentrated in stocks with small market capitalisations, although studies to adjust for this "size effect" have produced mixed findings. It is clear, however, that the excess returns have not been a product of assuming greater RISK. If anything the reverse is true: that a portfolio of low P/E ratio stocks will have less risk (as measured by STANDARD DEVIATION or BETA) than a high P/E ratio portfolio. The best explanation of this anomaly, therefore, is that investors generally underestimate the potential for earnings recovery from low P/E ratio stocks and overestimate potential future growth from those with high P/E ratios. To the extent that profits growth in companies is random – that is, unforeseen factors cropping up mean that few companies can grow their earnings at a consistent rate year in, year out – this is a logical conclusion. (See EFFICIENT MARKET HYPOTHESIS.)

M

MARCHE A TERME DES INSTRUMENTS FINANCIERS

The Paris market in FINANCIAL FUTURES, which is owned by the same company that runs the PARIS BOURSE and the Paris traded OPTIONS market, MONEP. The Marché à Terme des Instruments Financiers (MATIF) was founded in 1986 and trades contracts on a screen-based system, which replaced its trading floor in 1998. The advent of the euro meant that the MATIF lost its core product, a notional BOND futures contract based on French government TREASURY BONDS, which had accounted for about half its trading. As a result, trading volumes suffered in 1998 and 1999. Trading in futures based on the CAC 40 INDEX of leading French shares now dominates the MATIF's business, although the market has introduced a range of bond and interest-rate products based on the euro.

MARCHE DES OPTIONS NEGOCIABLES DE PARIS

Paris's TRADED OPTION market, founded in 1987, which trades options by both OPEN OUTCRY and a computer-assisted order book. The Marché des Options Négociables de Paris (MONEP) offers contracts on the CAC 40 INDEX of leading French companies, as well as options in the shares of over 30 major companies.

MARK TO MARKET

Basically, the daily adjustment to the value of an investment trading account to reflect changes in the market prices of components of the account. The term is most often used in FUTURES trading, although it applies equally when someone deals in cash securities using partly borrowed money. If the market value of the assets pledged to the account falls beyond a certain level, the trader will have to make further pledges. In the futures markets trading accounts are marked to market every day, sometimes within a day's trading if price movements are especially volatile. Traders then have to make good any margin commitments before the start of the following day's trading or face liquidation of the account.

M

MARKET MAKER
A dealer on the LONDON STOCK EXCHANGE who is willing to make continuous markets in the stocks in which he is registered to trade as principal. In return for taking the risk of being the market's wholesaler, market makers get various privileges. Most usefully, they can delay revealing large positions in stocks thus giving themselves time to unwind them, and they can sell STOCK they do not own. As such, they have pretty much the same function as stock jobbers, which existed until London's BIG BANG in 1986. However, market makers' privileges are increasingly under pressure as London moves towards a market that operates more like a European-style bourse, where bargains are matched directly between buyer and seller, and less like the system of competing market makers, as used by NASDAQ.

MATIF
See MARCHE A TERME DES INSTRUMENTS FINANCIERS.

MERGER ACCOUNTING
UK terminology for POOLING OF INTERESTS accounting when two companies are put together.

MEZZANINE FINANCE
Various types of finance which, in terms of RISK AND REWARD, bridge the gap between EQUITY and bank debt in the financing of a business. Mezzanine finance was developed in the United States in the 1960s, but received a big boost in the 1980s as the number of business deals using lots of LEVERAGE expanded rapidly. The aim of using mezzanine capital to finance a venture is to reduce the overall cost of capital while keeping the ownership rights tightly held. However, mezzanine finance often comes with an "equity kicker". This might take the form of warrants attached to loans or simply loans which are convertible into ordinary shares. Alternatively, straight loans may have a kicker which gives them extra interest if the business's profits cross a threshold.

M

MONEP
See MARCHE DES OPTIONS NEGOCIABLES DE PARIS.

MONEY MARKET FUND
A MUTUAL FUND which puts its capital into short-term money market assets, such as bank certificates of deposit, Treasury bills and commercial bills. In so doing, money market funds generate higher interest returns than bank savings accounts from which they suck deposits. First introduced in the United States in the early 1970s, when interest rates were particularly high, money market funds have been successful at attracting money. Savings in them rose from $244 billion at the end of 1985 to $717 billion at the end of 2000, according to Lipper Analytical Services.

MORTGAGE
The legal agreement in which one party (the mortgagee) agrees to make a loan and in return for which the borrower (mortgagor) agrees to pledge specific assets as security against the loan.

MUTUAL FUND
Also known as an open-end fund and in the UK as a UNIT TRUST. Mutual funds are the pooled funds, mostly investing in ordinary shares, whose success in attracting capital to manage has been notable. In the United States the amount of money invested in mutual funds rose from $495 billion at the end of 1985 to over $5,000 billion by the end of 1999; a compound annual growth rate of 18% during a period when the value of US stockmarkets, as measured by the S&P 500 INDEX, compounded annually at 15%. The picture in the UK was similar, where at the end of 1999 over £250 billion was under management in unit trusts. The key characteristics of mutual funds are as follows.

- There is no secondary market in the shares (units) of a mutual fund. Someone who wants to invest in a mutual fund does so by buying new shares in the fund, which consequently expands in size. Conversely, investors can only sell shares back to the fund, which shrinks when this happens. Hence the term "open end".

- These transactions take place at the per share value of the fund's investments less various administrative charges. This is feasible because in the main mutual funds hold marketable securities which can be readily valued as they trade on a recognised stock exchange. It gives a mutual fund an important edge over a CLOSED-END FUND, whose shares usually trade at less than their net asset value.

- Mutual funds are typically formed by a firm that specialises in investment management. The founding firm appoints a board of trustees to look after the interests of the shareholders (known as unit holders in the UK). In particular, the trustees appoint a management company to run the fund's investments. Most often it is the firm that launched the fund in the first place. The managers are remunerated by fees charged on new units when sold (the "load" fee) and by annual fees charged against the fund's income or capital.

- By investing in many securities, mutual funds can spread their risk. This is particularly important for small investors, who may not have the resources to buy a diversified portfolio themselves. The rules under which they operate, however, limit this goal because if they want to keep their tax benefits, mutual funds must remain fairly fully invested in their chosen medium. In the United States, for example, mutual funds must earn at least 90% of their income from holding securities. Consequently, they may be particularly vulnerable to falling stockmarkets.

- Mutual funds pay no taxes on the income they receive, or on the capital gains they realise. This is logical, since the liability to tax falls upon those who own the mutual fund shares. There is a caveat, which is that in order to qualify for tax-exempt status, funds must distribute most of the income they get (90% in the United States and 100% of income after costs in the UK, for example). They must also, incidentally, hold a diversified portfolio of assets. In the United States no more than 25% of a fund's assets can be in a single investment and for half a fund's portfolio no more than 5% of assets can be in the securities of a single issuer.

The key to making money in stocks is not to get scared of them… Every year finds a spate of books on how to pick stocks or find the winning mutual fund. But all this information is useless without the will power.
Peter Lynch, *Beating the Street*

NASDAQ

Short for National Association of Securities Dealers Automated Quotation System. Measured by the market value of the companies listed on the exchange, NASDAQ is now the world's second biggest stockmarket behind the NEW YORK STOCK EXCHANGE (NYSE). At the end of 1999, its market value was $5,036bn compared with $11,160bn for the New York exchange. However, the value of stocks traded on NASDAQ is greater than that of the NYSE. In February 2000, stock worth $1,827 billion was traded on NASDAQ compared with $855 billion on the NYSE.

NASDAQ owes much of its recent success to investors' demand for technology stocks, a high proportion of which have their shares listed on the exchange. Thus, for example, Cisco, Microsoft and Intel, three of the world's biggest companies by market capitalisation, have their only listing on NASDAQ. Young technology companies are persuaded to get their initial listing on NASDAQ because of its comparatively light listing requirements and to maintain them when they have grown because of its low listing costs.

The market was introduced in 1971 to replace a telephone-based market between members of the NASD, a self-regulatory body of dealers and market makers. It is still referred to as the United States's OVER-THE-COUNTER (OTC) stockmarket, which is true to the extent that NASDAQ has no trading floor and dominates OTC trading. But many small stocks are still traded outside the NASDAQ system by NASD members. Trading is done by over 500 market makers, who compete to make markets in over 5,000 issues via a screen-based system of competing quotes. All listed shares must have at least two market makers; the average number of market makers per stock is 11 and some of the bigger stocks have over 40 market makers. Despite this, NASDAQ has been criticised for the lack of competition among market makers in the prices they offer, particularly for SMALL CAP STOCKS.

NET PRESENT VALUE

A net present value (NPV) calculation answers the question: what will be the profit or loss measured in today's money values of an investment opportunity for a given DISCOUNT RATE? If the answer is positive then the present value of all the future cash inflows will be more than all the outflows. In other words, the investment will be profitable.

For example, assume a company is considering a capital project which would entail the following, net of tax cashflows:

Year	Cashflow ($m)
0	−20
1	−2
2	2
3	6
4	10
5	15

The project's viability will depend on the discount rate that the company chooses to express the net cashflows in today's values. If it were 8% then the project would generate a $2.2m profit, but if it were 12% then it would be a $1.1m loss. As such, a NPV calculation is similar to an INTERNAL RATE OF RETURN calculation. The latter simply finds the discount rate which would reduce the cashflows to zero. In this example it is 10.6%.

NET WORTH

The value of a company to its ordinary shareholders as recorded in its BALANCE SHEET. The residual amount left over from a schedule of the company's assets after deducting all the claims on the business which rank ahead of those of the ordinary shareholders. Also known as EQUITY, net assets, or net book value.

NEUER MARKT

A stock exchange launched in March 1997 by the DEUTSCHE BORSE as part of the FRANKFURT STOCK EXCHANGE for trading shares in technology companies. The Neuer Markt has had a successful start and by early 2000 over 200 companies, of which more than 30 were non-German, had an exchange listing. These had an aggregate market value of over $85 billion. The Neuer Markt will lose its identity if and when the planned merger between DEUTSCHE BORSE and the LONDON STOCK EXCHANGE goes ahead because it will be subsumed into a tie-up with NASDAQ that would use the US market's brand name.

NEW YORK STOCK EXCHANGE

The world's biggest stock exchange. At the end of 1999 the market value of US domestic common stocks listed on the New York Stock Exchange (NYSE) was $11,160 billion. In comparison, the market value of NASDAQ, the second biggest, was $5,036 billion and that of the TOKYO STOCK EXCHANGE, the third biggest, was $4,325 billion.

The NYSE is incorporated in New York State as a non-profit corporation and is controlled by its 1,366 members, who elect a board of 24 directors (there are also three ex-officio directors). However, the growing threat of ELECTRONIC COMMUNICATIONS NETWORKS means that the NYSE needs to become a quicker-moving organisation. To that end, in 2000 the NYSE was considering changing its structure to that of a for-profit corporation, perhaps even listing its shares on an exchange.

Trading on the exchange works through a system of brokers and specialists. The former are the link between the investing public and the market. The latter have a dual role: matching existing buying and selling orders when prevailing prices allow; and buying and selling stocks for their own account when this is not possible.

As the world's biggest exchange, the NYSE lists blue-chip stocks and those companies which aspire to such status. It has listing requirements which, although less stringent than in the past, aim to ensure that those companies whose stocks have been listed are solid concerns. Similarly, most major overseas companies seeking a US listing go to the NYSE rather than the alternative exchanges.

N

NEW YORK STOCK EXCHANGE COMPOSITE INDEX
An index of the stockmarket values of 1,500-plus companies listed on the NEW YORK STOCK EXCHANGE. It began in 1966 with a base level of 50 as at December 31st 1965, but an older index was subsequently incorporated into it giving a continuous price history stretching back to 1939. It is calculated as a weighted average of the stockmarket values of its constituents, its value is continuously updated and, therefore, it is suitable for FUTURES contracts to be written against it.

NIKKEI 225
Also known as the Nikkei Stock Average, this stockmarket index remains the best-known measure of share values on the TOKYO STOCK EXCHANGE despite its limitations. The Nikkei 225, which was first published in 1950, is composed of 225 shares from the first section (that is, bigger stocks) of the Tokyo exchange. Like the DOW JONES INDUSTRIAL AVERAGE, it is calculated as the simple average of the prices of its 225 components with an adjustment made to the denominator to take account of stock splits.

As a student of human nature, I always have felt that a good speculator should be able to tell what a man will do with his money before he does it.
Bernard Baruch

NOISE TRADER
A catch-all term used to describe a stockmarket trader who buys and sells securities for all the wrong reasons. Such traders are, thus, caught up in the noise of the market, seduced into dealing by the gossip and phoney analysis that does the rounds in any big market. Paradoxically, however, they help to make the market efficient by their trading. If they were not around there would be far fewer trades and therefore it would be more difficult to maintain market efficiency (see EFFICIENT MARKET HYPOTHESIS).

NPV
See NET PRESENT VALUE.

NYSE
See NEW YORK STOCK EXCHANGE.

ODD-LOT THEORY

The stockmarket application of the notion that if you do the opposite of what the dumbest person in town is doing, then it is likely to be right. So when amateur investors who deal in odd lots (extremely small amounts of STOCK) buy, it is time to sell, and vice versa. The theory even devises its own index by expressing the ratio of odd-lot sales to odd-lot purchases. Research has shown that odd lotters are not quite as dumb as they are made out to be. Besides, the success of the MUTUAL FUND has undermined the theory because many small-time investors now make their stockmarket investments indirectly via this vehicle.

OEICS

See OPEN-ENDED INVESTMENT COMPANY.

OFEX

An OVER-THE-COUNTER stockmarket in London run by a MARKET MAKER, J.P. Jenkins. OFEX was founded in 1995 when the LONDON STOCK EXCHANGE scrapped a rule which allowed its member firms to trade unquoted securities by matching buyers and sellers. All securities traded under this rule subsequently got a quote on the exchange's new ALTERNATIVE INVESTMENT MARKET or moved to OFEX. At the end of 1999 shares in 191 companies were traded on OFEX and they had a combined market value of £2.9 billion.

OFFER PRICE

The price at which dealers will sell securities in the market. It is the higher of the two prices that they will quote for any security in which they make a market. (See also BID PRICE and SPREAD.)

ON-THE-RUN BOND

A term used to describe the bonds and notes most recently issued by the US Treasury. It is a benchmark security which is heavily traded and thus moves at finer rates than other Treasury securities.

O

OPEN-ENDED INVESTMENT COMPANY

A type of investment fund which is a cross between a CLOSED-END FUND and a MUTUAL FUND. It has a corporate structure, yet its share capital is variable, rising and falling as investors in aggregate are net buyers or sellers of its shares. Open-ended investment companies (OEICS, pronounced "oiks") are usually arranged as an umbrella fund with a series of subfunds that specialise in particular types of investments. This structure offers savers cheap switching among subfunds with none of the confusion caused by the bid and offer prices at which mutual fund shares are bought and sold.

OPEN-END FUNDS

See MUTUAL FUND.

OPEN INTEREST

Within a FUTURES market, the open interest is the number of outstanding contracts. But note that for every contract there is both a buyer and a seller. Therefore the open interest changes only when new LONG and SHORT traders are coming into the market, rather than if existing traders are simply closing out their positions. Thus open interest can be an indicator of market sentiment; for example, a simultaneous increase in both the SPOT PRICE of an asset and the number of open positions in it in the futures market would imply strong underlying demand.

OPEN OFFER

A cheaper way for a company whose shares are already listed on a recognised stock exchange to raise additional capital than through a RIGHTS ISSUE. This is because an open offer does not give existing shareholders PRE-EMPTION RIGHTS over the shares to be issued, thus saving administration costs and underwriting fees. The term "open offer" is a misnomer because the new shares are generally placed with institutional investors by the company's advisers. Existing shareholders usually have the right to claw back new shares at a rate determined by their existing holding. However, because an open offer will not depend on the approval of existing shareholders in a ballot, this right has no market value. In the UK, companies are generally restricted to increasing their issued share capital by no more than 15% a year through open offers and this power is subject to approval by shareholders annually.

OPEN OUTCRY

The way in which trading is carried out on many FUTURES and options exchanges. It is a continuous auction process, which takes place on the floor of the exchange among dealers, to buy and sell contracts. Although it looks chaotic, unruly even, it is an efficient way of trading, especially in less liquid contracts. It depends on dealers using a combination of shouting and hand signals to show whether they are buying or selling, what their price is and how many contracts they are dealing in.

Why do people forever try to link the economy with the stockmarket. Economics have nothing to do with timing – and timing is everything.
Joe Granville

OPTION

The best-known of all types of DERIVATIVES, an option gives the holder the right, but not the obligation, to buy or sell a specific amount of an ASSET, probably ordinary shares, at a specified price within a specific period. Correspondingly, a person who underwrites an options contract accepts the obligation to deliver or buy shares according to the terms of the contract. In return, the buyer of the contract pays that person a fee upfront.

Options are not new. They were introduced in London as far back as the early 18th century and, indeed, they were banned from the LONDON STOCK EXCHANGE from 1734 to 1860. However, their formal trading on exchanges has been confined to the last 25 years or so when they were introduced

O

first on the CHICAGO BOARD OF TRADE in 1973 and then on the London exchange in 1978. In London they are known as traded options to distinguish them from conventional options, which are basically OVER-THE-COUNTER contracts. A further confusion is that there are American-style and European-style options. However, most trading is in the American-style instrument, even in Europe. The difference is that the holder of an American-style option can exercise the right to buy or sell the underlying STOCK at any time before the contract expires; with a European-style option the right to exercise comes only when the contract expires.

Options are either CALL OPTIONS or PUT OPTIONS. Calls give the holder the right to buy shares at a specific price; puts give the right to sell shares. Contracts are standardised so that in the UK, where share prices are generally smaller, one contract gives rights over 1,000 shares and in the United States a contract gives rights over 100 shares. In both the UK and the US, option contracts have the same pattern of expiry cycles. So, for example, the cycle beginning in January will have contracts which expire in April, July and October. The other cycles are: February, May, August, November; and March, June, September, December. All stocks which have traded options will be allocated to one of these cycles. This means that the maximum term of any option contract is nine months. However, in the US there are shorter, in-fill cycles so that leading stocks will have options contracts ending almost every month of the year.

Options are banded together in "series", which are defined by their expiry date and their EXERCISE PRICE. For example, a company's January 110 calls would be one series and its April 110 calls would be another. Initially, 12 series would be introduced for each underlying security, six for the calls and six for the puts. Within each group of six, three series would be for contracts above the prevailing price of the underlying security (one for each expiry date) and three below it. Then further series would be introduced as the price of the stock shifts, which is why the options pages of the financial press can quote so many series of options in a stock at any one time.

OPTIONS PREMIUM

The amount of cash that the buyer of an options contract pays and a seller (or WRITER) receives. In the market premiums are quoted on a per-share basis, but contracts are actually sold for lots of 1,000 shares (100 in the United States). So if a premium is quoted at 30p, a buyer pays £300 plus dealing costs. The premium itself can be analysed into two components: its INTRINSIC VALUE and its TIME VALUE (or speculative value).

ORDINARY SHARE

The security that companies issue in return for high-risk capital. Such capital is high-risk because it ranks behind other forms of capital in its claims on the income and assets of the corporation. The RISK, however, is limited to the value of the ordinary shares; that is, if the business fails, creditors and owners of other types of capital can make no claim on the shareholders beyond the funds they already have in the business. The corollary to risk is that ordinary shares carry unlimited potential for gains because other forms of capital have only fixed claims on the business. Shareholders also have ownership rights. They can vote directors in and out of office, approve their own dividends, change the nature of the company, even liquidate it if they wish. Most of the time these rights are more theoretical than real, but if sufficiently motivated, shareholders can exercise them.

OTC

See OVER THE COUNTER.

OUT OF THE MONEY

In options, a CALL OPTION is out of the money when the market price of the shares it can buy is lower than the price at which the options contract can be exercised. For example, if a company's shares trade at 100p, then options to buy the shares at 110p and 120p would be out of the money, although an option to buy at 90p would be IN THE MONEY. For a PUT OPTION, which is the right to sell shares at a specific price, the opposite is the case. A put option is out of the money when the market price is higher than the price at which the option can be exercised.

OVER THE COUNTER

A generic term used to describe trading in securities by any means other than on a recognised stock exchange. The term still carries a degree of disparagement, but this is wholly misplaced since globally the volume of over-the-counter (OTC) trading now dwarfs anything done on a stock exchange. This is in large part owing to the success of the London-centred EUROBOND market, where the average daily value of securities traded is over $20 billion. In comparison, the equivalent figure for the NEW YORK STOCK EXCHANGE, the world's biggest exchange, is about $10 billion. In the United States most government and municipal bonds are traded over the counter, and its second biggest stockmarket, NASDAQ, is essentially an OTC market. These successes, and the fact that the LONDON STOCK EXCHANGE effectively became an OTC market when it abandoned its trading floor in the late 1980s, make the distinction between OTC and exchange-traded securities increasingly irrelevant.

PAC-MAN DEFENCE

A tactic used by a company's management when facing a hostile takeover bid from another company. It comprises countering with a takeover bid for the original aggressor. The tactic is named after a video game of the 1980s in which all characters have to swallow their opponent or be consumed themselves.

PARI PASSU

Literally, with equal ranking. A phrase used in corporate documents to indicate that new shares issued by a company carry the same rights over income and assets as existing shares.

PARIS BOURSE

Helped by a fully computerised trading system, an innovative DERIVATIVES market and an ambitious privatisation programme by the French government, the Paris Bourse has been one of the world's fastest growing stockmarkets in recent years. By market value of the stocks quoted it is Europe's second largest behind London. At the end of 1999 the market value of its domestic equities was $1,437 billion. Its trading system, CAC, modelled on that used on the Toronto Stock Exchange, was introduced in January 1986 and has since been upgraded. In January 1991 France's six regional exchanges were merged into the Paris Bourse. In 2000 the bourse announced its intention to merge with the Amsterdam and Brussels stock exchanges to form EURONEXT. The order-driven computerised system stacks orders in a pre-trading session according to price limit. All buy orders for a security above its market price and sell orders below the market price are automatically executed. Thereafter orders are executed to the extent that matching bargains are available. Simultaneously, market prices of stocks are automatically calculated by the system and it arranges the flow of orders continuously through the trading day.

PAYBACK PERIOD

The length of time that it takes for an investment to generate sufficient cumulative CASHFLOW to pay back its cost. It is a simple measure, mostly used by companies to evaluate capital spending projects. Adjusting the cashflow by applying a DISCOUNT RATE to account for RISK can make it more useful.

PEP

See next entry.

PERSONAL EQUITY PLAN

A tax-break scheme introduced in 1987 in the UK to encourage "popular capitalism". Personal equity plans (PEPs) sheltered shareholdings from capital gains and income taxes. In return for the tax breaks PEP schemes required that funds were invested mainly in EU-domiciled companies and there were strict limits on the amount that could be invested in each tax year. PEPs were abolished at the end of the 1998/99 tax year.

P/E RATIO

See PRICE/EARNINGS RATIO.

POINT AND FIGURE CHART

An unusual way of plotting the price changes of an investment because the horizontal axis plots time, but not in specific regular intervals. The aim is to find areas where lots of price changes are compressed into a short period as this is supposed to presage a price break-out of the investment concerned. Only significant changes are plotted at all; say, when the price of the investment moves by 10p. As long as the changes are in the same direction they are stacked vertically, usually using X for an upward move and O for a fall. When the direction of movement switches, as well as changing the sign (from X to O or vice versa) the plots are shifted one column to the right. Thus when the price oscillates up and down the chart is stretched out horizontally, indicating that all-important break-out.

Point and figure chart

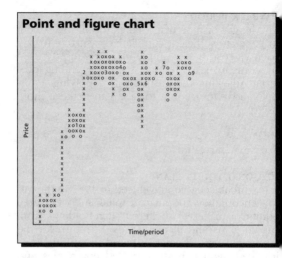

POISON PILL

A device, somewhat euphemistically called a shareholders' rights plan, which aims to protect a company from a hostile takeover bid. It is a legal contract giving shareholders of a target company rights, which, if exercised, would make the takeover of the company prohibitively expensive. The most familiar variant of the plan gives shareholders in the target company the right to buy up substantial numbers of new shares at a big discount to the market price in the event of a hostile bid. Since they were introduced in 1985, poison pills have swept corporate America and more than two-thirds of companies in the S&P 500 INDEX have adopted them. However, they are criticised for depressing the share price of companies and keeping inefficient managements in office. As a consequence, several large companies have scrapped theirs.

POOLING OF INTERESTS

A method of accounting for the merger of two companies that has the prime advantage that the transaction creates no accounting GOODWILL (which would have to be amortised against profits) and that the distributable reserves of both companies are available for future distribution to stockholders. However, in order to qualify for pooling of interests, various criteria have to be met; in particular, that shareholders of the two companies concerned continue their shareholdings as before, but on a combined basis.

PORTFOLIO THEORY

Investors intuitively know that there is a trade-off between RISK and return (that is, the greater the rewards they seek the bigger the risks they have to take and vice versa). It is equally intuitive that diversifying investments reduces risk because within a portfolio the value of some holdings will go up as others go down. The aim of portfolio theory is to provide a mathematical framework to explain how and why this happens and from there to make predictions for expected returns for portfolios in the real world.

The theory was originally formalised by Harry Markovitz in the early 1950s. He began by defining risk as the variability of returns from an average and proved that risk within a portfolio was not simply the weighted average risk of the portfolio's components, but that it could be reduced to less than the weighted average by means of diversification. Simultaneously, however, the returns on the portfolio would always be the weighted average of the components' returns. The implications of this were substantial: it is not only diversification that matters, but also how you diversify. Thus was born the idea of an EFFICIENT PORTFOLIO, one that produced the greatest returns for a specific level of risk or carried the least risk for a given return. So there must be an efficient portfolio for every increment of risk or return, giving rise to the concept of the EFFICIENT FRONTIER, the line on a chart which joins up all the efficient portfolios across the risk or return spectrum.

Simplifying Mr Markovitz's model was the next stage in the development. He arrived at a portfolio's risk or return trade-off by calculating how every pair of investments in a portfolio moved in relation to each other. This required a formidable amount of work. It was also unnecessary because it was increasingly clear that stocks, to which the theory was largely applied anyway, moved up or down in relation to the whole market as much as in relation to each other. So it was sensible to use the relation between a stockmarket index and each STOCK as the basis for calculating risk. This produced the SINGLE INDEX MODEL as a way of generating efficient portfolios; a method which involved much less work and produced portfolios similar to the full Markovitz workings.

Nowadays the single index model is used to work out efficient portfolios with many components. But where few components are involved, for example in allocating funds across the world's major stockmarkets, the Markovitz model remains the preferred choice because it examines the relationship between each pair of investments in the portfolio. (See also CAPITAL ASSET PRICING MODEL and CAPITAL MARKET THEORY.)

PRE-EMPTION RIGHTS
The rights of shareholders to maintain their proportionate ownership of a company. Thus when a company has a RIGHTS ISSUE, shareholders must be offered their pro-rata entitlement to new shares, which, consequently, have a market value that can be realised. However, in both the United States and the UK, especially the former, pre-emption rights are being eroded. In the United States the SECURITIES AND EXCHANGE COMMISSION, which regulates all STOCK issues, has not insisted that new stock be offered to existing stockholders when a corporation can raise new capital more cheaply by another means. The time and work involved in rights issues means that they are an expensive way of raising capital. Meanwhile, in the UK it looks increasingly likely that the competition authorities will decide that the way in which investment banks and investing institutions share out the underwriting commissions on rights issues is a cartel that should be broken up.

PREFERENCE SHARE

Technically part of the EQUITY capital of a company, thus carrying limited ownership rights, a preference share is better analysed as a hybrid form of debt. Its claims on a company are for a fixed DIVIDEND every year which, if not paid, usually accrues until it can be, and for repayment of its par value in the event of a winding up. Preference shareholders rank behind holders of debt in their claims, but ahead of the holders of ordinary shares. Generally, preference shares carry no voting rights, but this can change in some circumstances, usually if their dividends are in arrears. Increasingly they are issued with rights to convert into ordinary shares, in which case they usually have a fixed term before being repaid. Such shares can be valued as convertibles. Still, the majority of preference shares in issue are irredeemable and, therefore, given the fixed nature of their income, can be valued by grossing up the annual income by the required rate of return.

PREFERRED STOCK

See PREFERENCE SHARE.

PREMIUM

This has a variety of meanings within the world of investment, but the two most important are as follows:

- It is what the buyer of an options contract pays to acquire the contract.
- It means that one figure is in excess of another. For example, a CLOSED-END FUND's ordinary shares would be at a premium to the fund's net assets per share if they traded in the market for more than the BALANCE SHEET value of the attributable assets per share.

PRICE/EARNINGS RATIO

A ubiquitous investment tool for analysing the cheapness or expensiveness of ordinary shares. The success of price/earnings ratios (P/E ratios) derives from two things: their utter simplicity – the ratio is just the price of a share divided by a measure of its attributable earnings; and the intuitive ease with which they can be handled – a high P/E ratio implies that the market expects faster-than-average future growth from a share, and a low P/E ratio implies the opposite. However, this means that every tip sheet and investment analyst who can think of nothing better uses a low P/E ratio as a reason to recommend buying a share.

In practical terms investment analysts use P/E ratios to make comparisons between shares and the whole market or, more likely, between a share and its peer group. Thus utilities, for example, have traditionally traded on a ratio below the market average. The test of whether the shares of a utilities group are cheap, therefore, is not how they are rated in relation to the market (they will almost certainly be lower), but whether they will have a low P/E ratio relative to their sector. To determine this, analysts must look not at current earnings but at future earnings. The trouble is they rarely look far enough because the P/E ratio, like its close cousin the DIVIDEND DISCOUNT MODEL, is basically a discounting mechanism. Thus it reflects the present value that the market gives to all the future EARNINGS and dividends that a company will generate.

To explain, assume that a company is expected to pay a dividend of 10.5p per share for a full year; that its dividends are expected to grow constantly at 5% a year; and that an investor requires a 12% annual return from holding the shares. The constant growth dividend discount model would value such shares at 150p each by dividing the 10.5p DIVIDEND by the difference between the 12% required rate and the 5% expected growth rate. The sum is $10.5 \div (0.12 - 0.05)$.

This basic model can be adapted to calculate the appropriate P/E ratio by applying the company's expected earnings to the equation. Assume earnings are forecast to be 20p. Then the P/E ratio sum becomes $(10.5 \div 20) \div (0.12 - 0.05)$.

(See Appendix 5 for the algebraic formula.) This works out at 7.5 times earnings, which squares with the dividend discount model's valuation of 150p since 7.5 times 20p equals 150p.

These workings provide a basic model, but one which is especially sensitive to changes in the bottom-line variables, which themselves are always arrived at fairly subjectively. If the gap between the required rate and the expected dividend growth rate narrows, then the P/E ratio – and implicitly the share price – rises enormously and vice versa.

So P/E ratios have their uses, even if they are a limited tool. Nevertheless, not enough thought is given to the idea that the P/E ratio simply reflects the correct value of a share instead of the assumed notion that the search for the correct P/E ratio drives the share price.

Of the maxims of orthodox finance, none, surely, is more anti-social than the fetish of liquidity, the doctrine that it is a positive virtue on the part of investment institutions to concentrate their resources upon the holding of "liquid" securities.
John Maynard Keynes, *The General Theory of Employment Interest and Money* (1936)

PRICE-TO-BOOK RATIO

The ratio between the market price of an ORDINARY SHARE and the BOOK VALUE per share. Thus it is a measure of the value that the market awards to the shareholders' funds employed in a business. The higher the ratio then implicitly the more highly the market rates the company and the better are its prospects. This may be because investors believe that the true value of its assets are much higher than shown in its books, or that the likely future growth in EARNINGS will be sufficient to merit a high price-to-book ratio.

Alternatively, a low ratio may be particularly interesting to a follower of VALUE INVESTING because, in an extreme case where the stock price is below book value, investors are getting more than a pound of book value for every pound of stock they buy. The test will be whether the market knows something that individual investors do not when it values the stock so low.

The ratio is also applied across the whole stock-market as an indicator of cheapness or expensiveness. For example, the price-to-book ratio for the s&p 500 INDEX has historically been in the range of two to four times. However, by early 2000 it had risen to over six times, a level that arguably made the index look very expensive.

PROFIT AND LOSS ACCOUNT

Known in the United States as the income statement, it is that part of a company's financial accounts which shows the following:

- How much revenue was generated in a particular year.
- What costs were incurred in order to produce that revenue.
- What profits (surpluses) or losses (deficits) were left.
- How much taxation was charged on the profits.
- How much profit was left over for the shareholders.

Most important to grasp is that the profit and loss account is not just about the cash going in and out of the business. Rather, it is based on the ACCRUALS CONCEPT: that income and costs should be matched as far as possible with the period when they occur, not when the cash moved in or out. Thus some non-cash charges are regularly levied on the profit and loss account. Most significant are DEPRECIATION and the provision for taxes that will have to be paid in the future.

Correspondingly, some cash costs do not see the light of the profit and loss account when they are incurred, especially the cost of STOCK unsold at the end of the year and expenses deemed to be part of the capital cost of an ASSET in the making. Notable under this heading would be interest incurred on the borrowings for plant and buildings under construction, or the development costs of a major new product. Such expenses are often capitalised in the BALANCE SHEET. Reconciliation of these items with the company's underlying cash position should be made in the CASHFLOW statement. Nevertheless, good investment analysis demands that the accounting treatment of such items be critically assessed. In particular, changing policies for depreciation and capitalising costs can result in exaggerated profits. Similarly, big one-off items that occur in one year's profit and loss account should be stripped out and, if possible, averaged out over the years to which they really relate.

Our merchants and master manufacturers complain much of the bad effects of high wages in raising the price, and thereby lessening the sale of their goods both at home and abroad. They say nothing concerning the bad effects of high profits. They are silent with regard to the pernicious effects of their own gains. They complain only of those of other people.
Adam Smith, *The Wealth of Nations*

PROGRAM TRADING

Since the stockmarket crash of October 1987, program trading has been singled out as a cause of much of the instability on the world's major stockmarkets, especially Wall Street. The claim is difficult to prove, although clearly one type of program trading, INDEX ARBITRAGE, can cause sudden sharp movements in STOCK prices when positions are unwound. Program trading, however, is a more generic term for a variety of stockmarket strategies which embrace the aim of automatically rebalancing the weightings of assets in an investment portfolio through the use of options, FUTURES and the underlying securities. As such, it is not in itself inherently destabilising. However, it is monitored closely and in 1999 consistently accounted for over 15% of trading done on the NEW YORK STOCK EXCHANGE, in many weeks rising above 20%.

PUT HEDGE

A popular strategy in options trading to insure a shareholding or an entire share portfolio against possible future losses while retaining the right to gain from possible future price rises. Basically, an investor buys put options whose value will rise in the event of a fall in the price of the underlying shares, thus cancelling out some or all of the losses depending on how far the holding is fully hedged. If the share price does not actually fall, then the PUT OPTION will expire worthless, but this can be seen as the cost of an insurance policy which was never used.

PUT OPTION

Buying put options fulfils the archetypal bearish strategy because puts give the owner of a put contract the right, but not the obligation, to sell a STOCK at a specific price within a specified period. So if someone thinks that the price of an ORDINARY SHARE will fall in the coming months then the right to sell the stock above its market price will have value and will become more valuable the further the stock's market price falls. Thus a put option is the mirror image of a CALL OPTION, although it is less intuitively easy to understand.

Take a simple example. Assume that the price of a share in a company stands in the market at 380p and a put option is available for 10p, giving the right to sell the share at 370p. A BEAR who buys this put must believe that the price of the share will fall below 360p (the 370p at which he has the right to sell minus the 10p cost of acquiring that right) before the option expires. If it does not, the bear will lose money, but his maximum losses will always be pegged at 10p no matter how high the share price rises. However, if the price does fall then the value of the put will rise as the share price falls.

Thus puts, as well as providing an insurance policy for someone who holds the underlying shares, also provide an attractive speculation through the LEVERAGE that they offer. In the admittedly oversimplified example, if the price of the share falls to 340p then the speculator using puts would have made 20p for an outlay of 10p, a profit of 100%. Alternatively, he could have sold the shares SHORT at 380p and bought them back at 340p, but this would have realised only 40p profit, or 12%.

QUALITATIVE ANALYSIS

That part of investment analysis, almost always of ordinary shares, which requires some element of subjectivity. The qualitative assessment of a corporation would include taking a view on the prospects for the industry in which it operates, the strength of its competition and the ability of its management.

QUANTITATIVE ANALYSIS

Crunching numbers in order to determine whether a proposed investment passes muster, rather than using qualitative judgments. In analysing a single company quantitative analysis would entail calculating various ratios from the PROFIT AND LOSS ACCOUNT, BALANCE SHEET and CASH-FLOW statements. To find a portfolio of shares the exercise would involve selecting those securities which pass various quantitative tests; sufficient DIVIDEND yield, high return on capital, low PRICE/EARNINGS RATIO might be a simple one. The identity of the investments is much less important than their ability to pass statistical tests. In practical terms, however, the distinction between qualitative and quantitative elements becomes blurred, although there is a case for saying that the qualitative aspects of an investment are revealed in the quantitative findings.

R&D
See RESEARCH AND DEVELOPMENT.

R-SQUARED
A statistic that quantifies the proportion of VARI-ANCE in a STOCK's return that can be explained by the variance in the return from the market of which the stock is a part. In CAPITAL MARKET THEORY, REGRESSION ANALYSIS is widely used to predict stock returns. However, such analysis can only predict returns on average and in the real world there is a wide dispersion around the average. So R^2 measures the degree of fit between the market's returns and the stock returns. The higher the R^2, the more of the stock's return is predicted by the market's return.

RANDOM WALK
A branch of the EFFICIENT MARKET HYPOTHESIS that has probably generated more hot air than any other part of PORTFOLIO THEORY. To say that STOCK prices move along a random walk is explicitly to insult those who believe in the merits of TECHNICAL ANALYSIS and implicitly to insult adherents of FUNDAMENTAL ANALYSIS. Random walk says that the day-to-day changes in the market price of a stock are random. Therefore, tomorrow's closing price, or any future price, cannot be predicted on the basis of past closing prices. When price-sensitive information arrives the stock price will rightly change, but the arrival of that news is entirely random. Therefore the stock's price follows a random walk around the stock's INTRINSIC VALUE.

The major consequence of random walk is that past patterns of stock price changes become irrelevant in trying to predict future prices. In other words, it is not possible to make excess returns from analysing price patterns; therefore technical analysis is not worth the effort. Furthermore, if price changes are random it becomes debatable whether fundamental analysis is worthwhile, since acting upon price-sensitive announcements by corporations would not generate excess returns in the long run (the successes and failures would even themselves out).

In spite of all this, it remains – and is likely to remain – unproven whether stock prices do follow a random walk. The only certainty is that the debate will continue.

REDEMPTION YIELD

See YIELD TO MATURITY.

REGISTERED SECURITY

A security that is recorded in the name of the owner on a register kept by the issuer or the issuer's agent. Dividends or interest are automatically paid to the owner and transfer of ownership can take place only with the owner's consent. Most shares are registered, as are government-issued bonds.

REGRESSION ANALYSIS

A major tool of economics which finds uses in investment analysis. Regression analysis is about using statistical techniques to test the relationship between two or more variables in a mathematical model and to discover, therefore, whether it is reasonable to infer that past relationships will hold good in the future. Consequently, it is rigorously applied to the major models of investment analysis: the BLACK-SCHOLES OPTION PRICING MODEL, the CAPITAL ASSET PRICING MODEL and the main branches of PORTFOLIO THEORY.

REINVESTMENT RATE

A crucial element in investment calculations that show a staggeringly big sum being generated from a comparatively small starting amount is the reinvestment rate chosen. This is the rate of return applied to the income that is produced by the capital. Clearly, the higher the reinvestment rate and the further the investment horizon, the bigger is the final sum.

For example, imagine that $1,000 is tied up for 20 years and it generates $100 of income every year, therefore $2,000 over the whole investment period. If that income is reinvested to obtain a return of 15% per year over the period then the total of income plus interest on the income will be $8,900; that is, $6,900 will have come from reinvesting and just $2,000 from the original income. However, if the reinvestment rate was only 5%, then the total sum would be $3,154, with just $1,154 coming from reinvested income. This is quite a contrast.

By using as the rate for reinvesting income the rate at which an investment fund's capital grows, massive future sums can be generated from modest starting amounts. This is a familiar marketing trick used for mutual funds. The question is whether they are available in the real world. Regular savings plans for managed funds mean that returns at least approaching the reinvestment rate are accessible, but for those investing directly in shares, attaining a reinvestment rate equal to the capital growth achieved might be another matter.

REPO

A sale-and-repurchase agreement between two parties, usually associated with using marketable government debt as security for the transaction. In the United States, for example, there is a massive repo market in US Treasury notes and bonds and in the UK a Bank of England-approved repo market was introduced in 1996. The seller of the STOCK effectively raises a loan which will be repaid with interest by repurchasing the stock at a predetermined price. The buyer has title to the stock, but contracts to deliver equivalent securities at the agreed date.

For investors a liquid repo market means they can cheaply finance positions in the underlying market for government stock. For example, an investor who buys $10m of ten-year Treasury notes can immediately sell the notes in the repo market to finance his purchase. Rates of interest are keen because the collateral is risk-free government debt. The person buying in the stock is termed "reversing in" to the security. If he instigated the transaction to cover a SHORT position in the cash market then, technically, the deal is not a repo but a "reverse".

For governments the attraction of a well-developed repo market, in which their debt effectively takes on the characteristics of cash, is cheaper borrowing costs. Central banks also use repos on their own account to influence interest rates in the wider economy. Either they sell marketable debt for future repurchase to drain funds out of the banking system and push up rates, or they temporarily buy in bonds in order to reduce rates.

> *Business. It's quite simple.*
> *It's other people's money.*
> Alexander Dumas

RESEARCH AND DEVELOPMENT

The costs that companies run up in developing new products and bringing them to the market. For some types of company, notably pharmaceuticals and electronics businesses, these are substantial costs, so how they are treated becomes a material issue. Mostly companies write them off against income as the costs are incurred. However, some treat research and development (R&D) costs as the development of a future income stream and therefore CAPITALISE them as an ASSET in their balance sheets.

RETURN ON CAPITAL

Arguably one of the most, if not the most, useful ratios in assessing the performance of a company. It should show the reward that a company generates from the capital that it uses. So just as a savings account paying a higher rate of interest is better than one paying a lower rate, then, other things being equal, a company generating a high return on capital is better than one generating a lower return. The trouble is things rarely remain the same, and the challenge with calculating return on capital figures that are both comparable across time and among companies is to use numbers that are consistent and sensible, particularly for the amount of capital employed.

The basic sum, however, is simple; it is a measure of profit expressed as a percentage of the capital employed to generate the profit. Take the following example.

	Year 2	Year 1
	£m	£m
Shareholders' equity	3,863	4,622
Preference shares	14	16
Long-term debt	1,156	1,512
Short-term debt	711	706
Deferred taxes & allowances	578	529
Capital employed	**6,322**	**7,385**
Average capital employed	6,854	
Average equity employed	4,243	
Operating profit before interest	1,017	
Net profit after taxes	539	
Return on capital (%)	14.8	
Return on equity (%)	12.7	

These points are worth noting.

- The capital employed – £6,322m in year 2 and £7,385 in year 1 – is the gross amount of shareholders' EQUITY plus interest-bearing capital; that is, short-term creditors which have no explicit cost are excluded.
- The return on capital is profits before interest and taxes as a percentage of the capital employed.
- The equity employed is just the ordinary shareholders' interest in the business (that is, it excludes the preference capital shown in the table).
- Return on equity is profits after interest, taxes and preference shareholders' dividends as a percentage of equity employed.
- Both ratios are based on "average" capital employed; that is, the mid-point between the two years. So in this example, return on capital is calculated as £1,017m as a percentage of £6,854m and return on equity is £539m as a percentage of £4,243m.
- Return on capital could be adjusted so that loan capital gets the same tax treatment as equity; that is, the interest is no longer tax deductible. This helps comparisons between companies with differing levels of debt.
- The amount of capital employed can be

calculated from using either side of the
BALANCE SHEET.

- Many further adjustments can be made, but
the golden rule is to be consistent.

REVERSE YIELD GAP
See YIELD GAP.

RIGHTS ISSUE
A means by which a company raises new capital,
most often EQUITY but it can be convertible capital.
The essential principle behind a rights issue is that
existing shareholders in the company have the
right to maintain both their proportionate voting
power and their proportionate share of the
company's profits and assets. Thus the new
capital is offered to them first. This brings problems caused by the time and effort involved in no-
tifying all shareholders and giving them sufficient
time to decide if they want to take up the issue. As
time equals money, then rights are criticised as an
expensive way for a company to raise new capital
(see PRE-EMPTION RIGHTS). However, when managements do use rights issues (and they remain the
major way in which companies in the UK raise
new equity) they still do their best to persuade
shareholders that they are getting a good deal.

In fact, rights issues neither create nor destroy
value for shareholders, whether they accept the
issue or not. Take the following simple example.
A company offers shareholders one new share at
300p for every three shares they already own
(assume that the market price of existing shares is
350p). This means that for every three shares
(market value £10.50) that shareholders own, they
have the right to add another for £3. They have a
choice. Either they can make a pro-rata investment
of £3 for each new share, bringing their holding to
four shares with a value of £13.50 (£10.50 plus £3);
or they can keep their three shares and sell the
rights to the fourth in the market. If they opt for
the latter course, then, other things being equal,
the market value of their three "old" shares will fall
to £10.13 (three-quarters of £13.50), leaving them

37p SHORT on the value of their original holding. However, a conventional formula for valuing rights will produce the figure 37p as the value of the right to buy the new share for 300p. Thus the shareholders are back where they started with the option to use their £3 as they please.

The figures do not often work out quite so neatly in real life. This is partly because in the UK, although not in the United States, the sale of rights can create a tax liability. The details of the calculation also depend on how the market reacts to the news of the company's rights issue.

RISK
The flipside of return. If investors want anything more than the RISK-FREE RATE OF RETURN from an investment, they must bear some degree of risk. In other words, risk is the possibility that an investment will not turn out as well as expected. Within PORTFOLIO THEORY it is defined as the variability of returns, using either STANDARD DEVIATION or BETA, both of which are measures of VOLATILITY. Portfolio theory asserts that some risks can be eliminated by holding a diversified bunch of investments (UN-SYSTEMATIC RISK), but some cannot be diversified away (SYSTEMATIC RISK) because they are risks that are the concomitant of investing in a particular market.

RISK-FREE ASSET
An investment that carries a RISK-FREE RATE OF RETURN.

RISK-FREE RATE OF RETURN
The return on an investment which, for a given period, carries no RISK; the return is effectively guaranteed. This has important implications for PORTFOLIO THEORY. Imagine that a portfolio of assets whose returns are risky (that is, their final outcome is not known) is combined with a risk-free asset. Then, for a specified level of risk, the enlarged portfolio will always produce a superior return to a portfolio comprising only risky assets. This is because the overall return on any portfolio

will always be the average of the returns of the investments it contains weighted by their proportions, but the risk will comprise only the weighted average of the risky investments. This has to be so since the risk-free asset, by definition, carries zero risk.

The substitute for the risk-free rate of return is always the return offered on government debt for the time horizon under consideration. So if, for example, an investment analyst is considering the best investments with a five-year horizon the risk-free rate would be whatever is the YIELD TO MATURITY on five-year Treasury notes. Although the price of these notes would bounce around within the five-year period, the timing and amount of their dividends plus their value on redemption would be known with certainty in advance, therefore their risk-free rate of return could be calculated with equal certainty.

It takes patience, discipline and courage to follow the contrarian route to investment success: to buy when others are despondently selling, to sell when others are avidly buying.
John Templeton, founder Templeton Growth Fund

RISK AND REWARD

The conflict that lies at the heart of investment: if RISK is the possibility that an investment will not deliver the rewards expected, so these possible rewards must rise as the likelihood of their eventual delivery recedes. Thus investors can make worthwhile rewards only by taking risks. Logically this must be so. If there were big rewards to be made without taking risks then everyone would chase after them and by the process of ARBITRAGE they would be priced away.

Whether this is so in practice is debatable. The fact that year-in, year-out some professional investors can make excess returns indicates that they have found the ticket to a perpetual free lunch. Alternatively, they may simply be lucky. There are enough professional investors in the world with verifiable investment records for the notion to hold good that the few consistently successful ones are no more than the stockmarket equivalent of the people who always make the right call in a COIN-FLIPPING CONTEST.

RISK ARBITRAGE

A contradiction in terms, but nevertheless a term that came to have real meaning in the hectic world of corporate raiding in the 1980s. Risk arbitrage aims to make an automatic profit if an event takes place, but if the event does not occur there is no profit, hence the RISK. For example, if a company has made a hostile bid for another then a risk arbitrager (the colloquial term is "arb") might buy shares in the potential victim on the assumption that the bid has to be raised for it to succeed. Similarly, if the bidder is using its own shares to finance the potential deal, then the arb might sell the bidder's shares and buy the victim's with the aim of acquiring cheap shares in the combined corporation. If there are options in the shares of either or both corporations then the potential for arbs to demonstrate how smart they are becomes greater still.

> *I'm only interested in what we can lose. The downside risk is something I constantly hammer home to my people involved in acquisitions. I say: "Don't worry about how much you can make, how much can you lose?"*
> Lord White, co-founder, Hanson

RULE OF TWENTY

A useful little investment rule that says that the PRICE/EARNINGS RATIO of a stockmarket plus the inflation rate in the domestic economy should equal 20. So if the P/E ratio on the NEW YORK STOCK EXCHANGE were 16 times, the prevailing inflation rate should be 4% or thereabouts. For both the US and the UK EQUITY markets the rule works well (particularly in the case of the UK), thus providing a cheapness or expensiveness indicator for the markets. When the sum of the two variables is well short of 20, shares are cheap; when it is comfortably clear of 20 they are expensive.

It should be no surprise that the rule has credibility. If the inflation rate rises then interest rates are likely to follow suit, thus driving down the price first of bonds and then of equities. In other words, the market's P/E ratio will fall to compensate for the higher rate of inflation. Conversely, falling inflation and falling interest rates usually go together, signalling higher share prices. This is partly because low interest rates mean investors are willing to accept lower running returns and will therefore pay more for shares; and partly because they see more of their future returns coming from the higher share values which will flow from the increased economic activity engendered by low inflation.

The rule's limitation is that it predicates future market movements based on indicators of past performance; whereas in reality a sum of over 20 may be perfectly reasonable if, for example, a high inflation rate is expected to fall fast, bringing with it a rapid upturn in real corporate profits.

RULE OF 72

A rule of thumb that says how many years it will take for an investment to double for a given annual COMPOUND RETURN. The number of years is found by dividing the interest rate into 72. So an investment growing at 10% a year will take 7.2 years to double. Conversely, the equation can be rearranged to discover the rate of interest. If an investment doubles over five years, then its compound rate of growth has been 72 divided by five – 14.4%.

S&P 500 INDEX

The full name is the Standard & Poor's 500 Composite Index. As its name suggests, it is an amalgam of other stockmarket indicators produced by Standard & Poor's, a financial information provider: namely, the S&P Industrial Average (385 stocks), S&P Transportation Average (15 stocks), Utility Average (44 stocks) and Financials Average (56 stocks). It is successful as a measure of US stockmarket values and as a benchmark for measuring investment performance because it is broadly based (its constituents include stocks accounting for about 80% of the market value of those listed on the NEW YORK STOCK EXCHANGE) and it is a market value index. This means that its value is weighted by the stockmarket value of each of its constituents. A 1% change in the market value of Exxon, therefore, would have a much greater impact than a 1% change in the value of Apple Computer. Although it was started in 1957, the S&P 500's base value is 10 for the period 1941–43.

SCRIP ISSUE

An arrangement largely confined to the UK, in which a company will CAPITALISE some of its retained EARNINGS. It is purely a book-keeping exercise in which a lump of capital is moved from one part of shareholders' EQUITY to another. Say the equity in a company looks like this:

	£m
Ordinary shares (25p par value)	200
Retained earnings	600
Unrealised revaluations	400
Total	**1,200**

Then the directors of the company decide on a capitalisation issue of one for two (that is, for every two shares that shareholders own, they receive one new share). The transfer would have to come from retained earnings, which would mean issuing another 400m shares with a 25p par value and switching the

£100m needed to "pay" for the shares from retained earnings to ordinary shares. Thus after the exercise shareholders' equity would look like this:

	£m
Ordinary shares (25p par value)	300
Retained earnings	500
Unrealised revaluations	400
Total	**1,200**

It is important to realise that value has neither been created nor destroyed by the exercise. A shareholder with 10,000 shares in the company before the scrip issue would have a pro-rata claim on £120,000 of its NET WORTH. After the issue the shareholder's claim would still be £120,000; it would simply be divided among 15,000 shares and the per share value would have declined by one-third. Exactly the same would happen to the market value of the company's shares. If they traded at 600p each before the issue they would, other things being equal, fall to 400p afterwards.

However, this caveat provides the justification for scrip issues. Some research indicates that share prices perform well immediately after such an issue; possibly because the LIQUIDITY of the company's stock has improved, thus helping some investors to buy, or, more tenuously, simply by making the share price look more attractive because it is lower. The latter explanation does not stand up to examination, but this does not stop some interested parties claiming it, particularly those company bosses who describe such an issue as a BONUS ISSUE.

SEAQ
See STOCK EXCHANGE AUTOMATED QUOTATIONS.

SEATS PLUS
See STOCK EXCHANGE ALTERNATIVE TRADING SERVICE.

SEC
See next entry.

SECURITIES AND EXCHANGE COMMISSION

The watchdog that regulates the US securities industry. Like regulatory authorities in so many areas it is under-resourced, yet it has considerable powers and frequently uses them; most notably in recent years in the prosecution of Michael Milken and Ivan Boesky on insider dealing charges (see JUNK BOND). Both men got prison sentences; Mr Milken was fined $200m and ordered to pay $400m into a restitution fund, while Mr Boesky was fined $100m. This is not bad for an organisation whose first chairman was Joseph P. Kennedy (father of John F.), a notorious inside trader in the 1920s when such practices were not illegal. Indeed, the Securities and Exchange Commission (SEC) was established in 1934 in response to Wall Street's excesses in the 1920s. It derives its powers from the Securities Act 1933, which governs the issue of securities to the public, and the Securities Exchange Act 1934, which regulates stock exchanges (including options markets) and all those whose work is connected to them.

I want you to know that I think greed is healthy. You can be greedy and feel good about yourselves.

Ivan Boesky, to a class of business graduates
at University of California

SECURITY ANALYSIS

The book that gave rise to the discipline. Before BENJAMIN GRAHAM and David Dodd published their book, *Security Analysis*, in 1934 there was no formal analysis of the stocks and bonds that trade on the US capital markets. Now security analysis is a quasi-science with all the attendant jargon (although, happily, the book is not responsible for this); there is a Financial Analysts Federation and an Association of Investment Management and Research in the United States and an Institute of Investment Management & Research and a Securities Institute in the UK, which altogether have tens of thousands of members. The book, meanwhile, has been in print continuously since first being published. It remains a standard and down-to-earth work on the subject and is now into its fifth edition, which came out in 1988.

SECURITY MARKET LINE
The chart line that illustrates the idea that investors are rewarded only for the risks they take in relation to overall market risk (SYSTEMATIC RISK). As such, it is the linear representation of the CAPITAL ASSET PRICING MODEL.

SERIOUS FRAUD OFFICE
A UK government department that pursues major fraud cases and is as well-known for its spectacular failures as its successes, even though in the period 1998–2000 two out of three of the 447 defendants it has prosecuted in 200 cases have been convicted. Its highest-profile failures include the acquittal of 14 defendants in three trials involving an alleged £140m fraud over a rights issue by a UK quoted company, Blue Arrow; the acquittal of three defendants over an alleged £150m fraud on pension schemes connected with companies controlled by the late Robert Maxwell; and the acquittal of the principal defendant, George Walker, in a £164m fraud on creditors and shareholders of a leisure company, Brent Walker. Some of its successes have been criticised too, though for reasons beyond its control. Namely the light sentences given to those convicted in a case of share-price manipulation of a drinks group, Guinness, and a £58m fraud involving an insurance broker, Levitt.

The Serious Fraud Office (SFO), which was established in 1988, operates under powers in the 1987 Criminal Justice Act with a brief to investigate major and complex fraud cases where there is public interest and the alleged fraud exceeds £1m.

SETS
See STOCK EXCHANGE ELECTRONIC TRADING SERVICE.

SFO
See SERIOUS FRAUD OFFICE.

SHARPE RATIO

Named after William Sharpe, who won a Nobel prize for his work on financial economics, the Sharpe ratio measures the amount of return from an investment portfolio for a given level of RISK. It does this by dividing a measure of portfolio VOLATILITY (the STANDARD DEVIATION of its returns over a specific period) into the excess returns generated by the portfolio over the RISK-FREE RATE OF RETURN for the same period. The higher the resulting number, the better is the portfolio performance. This ratio, also known as the reward-to-variability ratio, is used to rank the performance of investment funds.

SHORT

The adjective that describes traders who have a position in a security that they do not own. In other words, they have committed to deliver STOCK at a specific price some time in the future and must buy in stock to fulfil their bargain. By definition therefore someone who is short of stock anticipates a fall in its price and is a BEAR (see LONG).

SHORT INTEREST RATIO

A measure of investor sentiment towards US common stocks, which is calculated monthly. It takes the total number of shares that have been sold SHORT and divides it by the market's average daily trading volume for the previous month. In other words, it expresses the number of days it will take for the market to work off its short position. The higher the ratio – the greater the number of days needed – the more bullish are the market's short-term prospects. This is so because even though the stocks were sold short in the hope of a fall in the market, whatever happens they have to be bought back in order to close out the short-sale contracts. Thus the ratio is an indicator of latent demand in the market. Investors' ability to HEDGE short positions using FUTURES or options means that the ratio has less relevance nowadays than in the past; even so, a ratio of above 4.0 for the NEW YORK STOCK EXCHANGE would be at the high end of the normal range and, therefore, a bullish signal.

SHORT SELLING

Selling something you do not own in the hope of buying it more cheaply in the future, thus making a profit. On the main US stock exchanges short selling remains popular and often accounts for approaching 10% of all bargains done on the NEW YORK STOCK EXCHANGE (although about half of this is generally done by specialists to meet buy orders). However, it is circumscribed by tight rules, in particular that short sales in a STOCK can be made only when the stock's most recent price change was up. Short sales are effected by borrowing stock from another party who still receives any dividends paid on the stock while the short sale remains in effect. Brokers require the seller to put up security against the sale, which is marked to market.

In the UK short sales used to be popular when shares were traded over a two-week accounting period for settling stock transactions. The abolition of these accounting periods effectively made short sales impractical, except for market makers, who sell short as part of their regular business.

SINGLE INDEX MODEL

The trouble with PORTFOLIO THEORY when it was formulated was that prodigious amounts of calculation were needed in order to find those portfolios of investments that provided the best trade-offs between RISK and return. This was because the key measure of risk was how far the returns on each pair of investments in a portfolio varied in relation to each other. The groundwork for a portfolio of 200 stocks, for example, would need 19,900 COVARIANCE calculations.

However, it became increasingly clear that in the real world of stockmarkets much of the price changes in a security depended on movements in the whole market, so a portfolio model was developed which related returns on shares to their sensitivity to a single market index, say the

S&P 500 INDEX of US stocks or London's ALL-SHARE INDEX. Basically, the single index model says that a security's return will comprise a constant return made irrespective of the market's returns plus the degree to which the security's own returns magnify or minimise the market's returns.

Say the constant return, called the share's ALPHA, was 8% a year, the market's return was 10% and the share's sensitivity to the market was 1.5 (that is, the share's returns were always 1.5 times the market's, up or down). Then the share could be expected to return 23% if the market rose 10%, but just 0.5% if the market fell 5%. The calculations are a bit more complicated than this, as the formula in Appendix 5 shows. But the single index model works well and greatly reduces the work needed to find the best combinations of shares. For the same portfolio of 200 shares there would need to be only 602 calculations all told.

SINKING FUND

The provision set aside for the repayment of a debt, most likely a marketable BOND. When the provision has been built up to sufficient levels the borrower can buy in the debt in the market. Effectively, therefore, the debt is paid off in instalments, giving the borrower greater flexibility. For the lenders (that is, those who own the bonds) the possibility of default is reduced.

SMALL CAP STOCK

Market shorthand for companies that have low stockmarket capitalisations. Small cap stocks are interesting because research in both the UK and the United States has shown that they produce better returns than bigger companies. As a rule of thumb, the excess returns increase as the market capitalisations get smaller. But because companies with low market capitalisations also often have a low share price, it is not always clear if the excess returns result from the market capitalisation or the share price. Studies have shown that both characteristics generate above-average returns.

It is more relevant to ask why this phenomenon persists even though it is well known. EFFICIENT MARKET HYPOTHESIS says that the extra returns should be priced away by profit-maximising investors. However, it is likely that the market is not particularly efficient at pricing small companies because it is not worthwhile for investment analysts to do the research on them that would produce a "correct" price. They may be more risky than big companies, although this does not show from the STANDARD DEVIATION of their returns. They may also carry greater risk of business failure as they are more vulnerable to swings in the economic cycle. Indeed, research into UK small cap stocks showed that their returns were well correlated with overall profits in the economy.

> *I was as badly caught as the next fellow. I was convinced the crash would start in Japan; that turned out to be an expensive mistake.*
> George Soros on the October 1987 crash, from
> *The Alchemy of Finance*

GEORGE SOROS

The man who famously "broke" the Bank of England when he took a massive position against sterling in 1992, thus helping to force the UK government out of a semi-fixed exchange rate mechanism with its EU partners. George Soros, a Hungarian-born New Yorker, set up the Quantum Fund, an offshore HEDGE FUND, which produced remarkable annual compound returns of over 30% between 1969 and 1999. His style was to take big, often interlinked, speculative positions using lots of LEVERAGE so that, say, a 1% favourable move in the yen would produce a 10% gain in the fund's NET WORTH. This approach sometimes caused the Quantum Fund to sustain savage losses. For example, it lost 32% after the stockmarket crash of October 1987. Even so, since its formation it had only one down year, 1981. In 2000 the $8 billion Quantum Fund signalled an end to its aggressive days and targeted lower investment returns for the future.

SOUTH SEA BUBBLE

One of the earliest, and arguably most infamous, episodes of share speculation gone mad. It featured the South Sea Company, a London company whose aim was to trade in Spanish South America in the early 18th century and whose confidence of success was such that it offered to swap all the British government's debt for its own shares. Encouraged by the British government, which was apprehensive that the French government was in the process of getting rid of its own debt by a similarly fraudulent scheme and therefore keen to do the same, and lapped up by a newly wealthy British public, South Sea Company shares surged from around £100 at the start of 1720 to £307 when the law was passed permitting the takeover of the national debt. Stimulated by further issues of partly paid shares at £300 and £400, the South Sea shares rose to £1,050 by June 24th 1720. By then rumours that the company's directors were selling leaked out. Coupled with the dawning realisation that the company's trading prospects were non-existent, the shares plummeted to £150 by the end of September.

SPECIALIST

A key player on the NEW YORK STOCK EXCHANGE (NYSE). The role of specialists is to ensure a continuous orderly market in stocks for which they have responsibility. Their function is twofold. When prevailing market prices allow, they match existing orders to buy and sell stocks, thus acting as glorified brokers. More importantly, however, when it is not possible to match orders automatically, they buy and sell for their own account, thus facilitating a continuous market and taking the concomitant RISK on themselves.

In exchange for assuming risk, they have a monopoly; no STOCK on the NYSE has more than one specialist. This fact often invites criticism, especially when markets fail under extreme conditions (for example, October 1987). In these circumstances the system of competing market makers, as used by NASDAQ, is cited as a better model. For the most part, though, the specialist system works satisfactorily. As evidence for this, the NYSE shows that virtually all transactions occur with either no price change in the security concerned or just the minimum change allowed by NYSE rules.

SPECULATIVE VALUE
See TIME VALUE.

SPECULATOR
A term of abuse directed at a market's participants when markets move in ways that are both strange and disadvantageous to the general public. More specifically, speculators perform a useful function. For a price they will assume RISK, much like an insurance company assumes the potential cost of a domestic mishap. In so doing, they also maintain a market's liquidity by buying when there is a surfeit of sellers and supplying the market's stock-in-trade when buyers are abundant.

SPOT PRICE
The price of an ASSET for immediate delivery; that is, as soon as the delivery mechanism used between the buyer and seller allows. It is usually used in the currency or commodity markets to distinguish between the price of goods for immediate delivery and the price for delivery at a specific time in the future.

SPREAD
The difference between the price at which a marketable security is bought and sold. Thus it is the wholesaler's, or MARKET MAKER'S, mark-up.

In options trading spread is the generic term that embraces a variety of strategies whose common characteristic is that the potential maximum profit and maximum loss is known at the outset of the transaction. This is because an investor places himself on both sides of the transaction and therefore, beyond certain movements in the price of the underlying STOCK, finds that the profits and losses from his positions cancel themselves out. Spread strategies fall into two categories.

- Money, or vertical, spreads where the investor takes advantage of the differing values given to options which have the same expiry date, but a different EXERCISE PRICE.
- Time, or horizontal, spreads where investors simultaneously buy and sell options contracts which are identical apart from their expiry dates, thus seeking to take advantage of the different rates at which TIME VALUE in options erodes.

For example, take a BULL call spread, the most popular variation on the theme. An investor buys a CALL OPTION with a low exercise price and simultaneously sells, or writes, a call option (that is, agrees to deliver stock) with the same expiry date but at a higher exercise price. The immediate effect is that he receives less premium income than the cost of the call he buys. But this would represent his maximum potential loss if the underlying stock price falls. This is so because if the stock price falls sufficiently he would not want to exercise his right to buy stock, but nor would he have to deliver stock at an even higher exercise price. If, however, the stock rises as hoped the call option would become increasingly valuable, but the profit derived from it would be pegged by the losses that would ensue from the call the investor had written at the higher exercise price.

STAG
Someone who buys shares in a new issue with the intention of selling for a profit as soon as dealings in the market begin.

STANDARD DEVIATION
The statistical measure without which PORTFOLIO

THEORY would not be as we know it today. The great merit of standard deviation is that it measures variations around an average in a way that is accessible to everyone. Take, for example, the performance figures shown in Appendix 2 for the world's leading stockmarkets. These show that from 1970 to 1999 the average annual change in the value of the S&P 500 INDEX was 11% and for London's ALL-SHARE INDEX it was 15%. On this basis, ignoring, for argument's sake, the effects of exchange rates, an investor would have preferred to have had a long-term holding in the All-Share Index.

However, the standard deviation of the All-Share at 31% was almost twice as high as the S&P, whose standard deviation was 16%. This puts a different complexion on things. Given that a normal distribution pattern shows that two-thirds of the time returns will be within plus or minus one standard deviation of the average, then two out of three of the All-Share's returns would have been within 46% and –16% and two-thirds of the S&P's would been within 27% and –5%.

Thus using standard deviation tells us that an investor who is reluctant to live with the possibility of uncomfortably large annual losses in return for the potential for big annual gains would prefer the comparatively quiet life offered by the S&P's returns. Given that portfolio theory is all about the trade-off between RISK and returns, standard deviation becomes a useful measure – more useful, incidentally, than VARIANCE, the statistical measure from which it is derived. Variance expresses deviation from the average in terms of the square of the unit measured, whereas standard deviation, which is the square root of variance, talks in terms of the actual units.

STOCK

A little word that is full of ambiguous meaning.

- In the UK it is often used as an abbreviation for GILT-EDGED STOCK and thence an abbreviation for all types of FIXED INTEREST SECURITY.

- Additionally in the UK it is used as a substitute for security.
- In the United States it is used as an abbreviation for COMMON STOCK.
- Within a company's BALANCE SHEET, stock is the UK equivalent of inventory in the United States, that is, the goods which a company processes in the expectation of making a profit.

They told me to buy this stock for my old age.
It worked wonderfully.
Within a week I was an old man.
Eddie Cantor

STOCKBROKER

The agent who buys and sells quoted securities on behalf of his clients and in return is paid a commission based on the value of the business done. As an agent the broker has a legal obligation to transact the business at the best possible price for the client. Increasingly, however, stockbrokers perform an array of functions, all related to investing in quoted securities. This may include fund management (managing clients' investment portfolios) and trustee services (looking after all the financial needs of wealthy clients). In addition, most of the world's major investment banks have stockbroking arms. In the case of some (for example, Merril Lynch in the United States and Nomura in Japan) the bank grew out of the broking arm. In other cases (for example, Banque Paribas in France) a broking arm was added to help distribute the securities generated from INVESTMENT BANKING functions.

STOCK EXCHANGE ALTERNATIVE TRADING SERVICE

The computerised price information service used on the LONDON STOCK EXCHANGE for shares that cannot support more than one MARKET MAKER, either because they trade infrequently or because they are quoted on London's ALTERNATIVE INVESTMENT MARKET. After an upgrade in June 1995, the service became officially known as SEATS PLUS.

> *'Tis a compleat system of knavery, that 'tis a trade founded in fraud, born of deceit and nourished by trick, cheat, wheedle forgeries, falsehoods and all sorts of delusions.*
> Daniel Defoe on stockbroking

STOCK EXCHANGE AUTOMATED QUOTATIONS

Introduced as part of BIG BANG on the LONDON STOCK EXCHANGE in 1986, Stock Exchange Automated Quotations (SEAQ), pronounced "See-ack", is the computerised system for distributing the bid and offer prices in shares and fixed-interest securities quoted by wholesalers (MARKET MAKERS). Within specified limits for the amount of STOCK, market makers are obliged to deal at the prices they quote on SEAQ. The system automatically highlights the best bid and offer prices quoted on a yellow strip on its screen.

STOCK EXCHANGE ELECTRONIC TRADING SERVICE

A share trading system introduced in 1997 by the London Stock Exchange to match bargains between buyers and sellers automatically, thus cutting out the exchange's middlemen – the MARKET MAKERS. Known as SETS, the trading system has been unpopular with both investors and market makers. It has not been extended to share trading in as many companies as originally planned and it will be scrapped if the merger between the London exchange and the DEUTSCHE BORSE, announced in mid-2000, is completed.

STOP LOSS

On the logic that any stockmarket investment has an element of gambling, a stop loss is a sensible and simple tactic which, if adhered to, will almost always limit losses in any situation. All it entails is an instruction to sell a security if its price falls below a pre-defined level. The major risk it carries is that in a chaotic market the stop-loss order may not be capable of execution near the level specified. Additionally, there is the potential for an opportunity loss if the security's price subsequently recovers. Even so, in high-risk options and FUTURES strategies, a stop loss is a prerequisite.

> *It requires a great deal of boldness and a great deal of caution to make a great fortune.*
> Nathan Mayer Rothschild

STRADDLE

A tactic used in options trading which would be employed by someone who expects the price of underlying shares to be volatile. Investors simultaneously buy a CALL OPTION and a PUT OPTION in a share which have the same EXERCISE PRICE and expiry date. Thus they can make money if the share price rises or falls. However, for them to profit, the share price has to move further in at least one direction than if they were just buying a call or a put. This is because they have to cover the cost of two contracts. Thus their break-even position has been extended.

Someone on the other side of the transaction must believe that the underlying share price will move little during the period of the contract. He simultaneously sells both a call and a put and, in market jargon, has written a "SHORT straddle". The advantage to the WRITER of the short straddle is that he receives two lots of premium income. Against that, he can lose money on both the call and the put if the price turns out to be especially volatile. In practical terms, he would probably have a STOP LOSS position on one side of the transaction to limit the potential losses in one direction.

STRIKE PRICE

See EXERCISE PRICE.

STRIPS

It seems common sense that if an investment bank strips the coupons from a BOND and sells them separately, then the word "strips" self-evidently describes the product. However, when the US

Treasury launched its version of stripped bonds it felt obliged to make an acronym of the word. Hence strips now stands for Separate Trading of Registered Interest and Principal of Securities. Take, for example, a 15-year TREASURY BOND. It could be carved up into 30 discounted securities, each of which would represent a claim on a future interest payment, and a 31st, which would be a claim on the principal on redemption. Effectively, therefore, 31 ZERO-COUPON BONDS would have been created, offering investors almost any maturity and all free from risk of default.

Strips were, in fact, the Treasury's response to an unofficial market in stripped government bonds. Merril Lynch, an investment bank, led the way with TIGRs, Treasury Investment Growth Receipts (or Tigers); Salomon Brothers, another bank, followed with CATS, Certificates of Accrual on Treasury Securities; and so the market (and the acronyms) grew. The success of bond stripping even persuaded the Bank of England to launch an official market into stripped GILT-EDGED STOCK, which began in 1997.

SWAPS

A DERIVATIVES product; a way in which borrowers or lenders of funds remove either the interest rate risk or the exchange rate risk, or both, from a transaction. Thus a company which had variable rate borrowings could remove its exposure to a rise in interest rates by arranging with a bank to swap its floating-rate payments for a fixed-rate payment, although clearly in doing so it is actually swapping one sort of RISK for another. The variations on the theme are enormous, including being able to buy the OPTION to take out a swap within a specific period: a swaption.

SYSTEMATIC RISK

If RISK is the possibility that investment returns will fail to reach expectations, then systematic risk comprises those components of overall risk that cannot be eliminated by allocating capital to a diversified portfolio of investments. Primarily this consists of market risk. An investment in a particular market must necessarily bear those risks that affect the whole market; if a stockmarket falls then most of the stocks that trade within it will suffer to some extent. Closely related to market risk is interest rate risk. Clearly, the short-term values of many investments will be depressed if interest rates rise. Similarly, the risk of inflation – the declining purchasing power of invested money – is difficult to escape. (See also UNSYSTEMATIC RISK.)

THE TAKEOVER PANEL

The UK's regulatory body that is concerned with the takeover of companies whose shares are held by the public. The panel was set up in 1968 in response to growing criticism of unfair takeover practices. Its brief is to ensure that all shareholders in a company in receipt of a takeover bid are treated fairly, according to the City Code of Takeovers and Mergers. Although it has no sanctions of its own, the panel's reputation for dispensing common-sense rulings speedily during the hurly-burly of a takeover means that it is a successful example of self-regulation.

TAX-EXEMPT SPECIAL SAVINGS ACCOUNT

The bottom rung of the tax-free savings and investment ladder in the UK introduced in 1991 and abolished in March 1999. A tax-exempt special savings account (TESSA) allowed anyone aged over 18 to earn interest tax-free from a savings account, provided they stuck to a few rules. The most important was that within specific annual limits no more than £9,000 could be deposited over the TESSA's five-year term.

TechMARK

A stockmarket index for listed technology companies introduced by the LONDON STOCK EXCHANGE in November 1999. TechMARK was created in response to investors' enthusiasm for high-tech companies and at the end of 1999 comprised 190 companies with an aggregate market value of £626 billion. The biggest concentration of value was within telecommunications companies, which accounted for 50% of techMARK's value, followed by pharmaceuticals companies, which accounted for 26% of its value.

TECHNICAL ANALYSIS

The branch of investment analysis that is sometimes ridiculed, yet survives and at times thrives. It is ridiculed because it is easy to grasp and requires no great intellectual effort. It survives because – who knows? – it might just work and it almost certainly helps give insights into the psychology of investors in a particular market.

The basic idea of technical analysis is that it makes price predictions based on published data – mostly prices, but also volume of business done – of a STOCK, commodity, market, whatever. By looking at past price/volume patterns and applying rules of thumb, "buy" and "sell" signals are generated for the present. It readily follows, therefore, that most technical analysis is done using charts because of the ease with which they can show trends. Technical analysis assumes that market prices are driven by factors which have more to do with the psychology of a market's participants than with changes in underlying economic values. Therefore it searches for trends, which are often self-reinforcing, and for signs of the tensions that mount before trends are broken. Support and resistance levels for a price thus become important.

Many investment analysts who criticise technical analysis unknowingly use technical techniques in their analysis; the ubiquity of computer-generated price charts ensures this. However, the credibility of technical analysis has never really been the same since the development in the 1960s of the EFFICIENT MARKET HYPOTHESIS and RANDOM WALK theory. Few people believe that even big, liquid markets are truly efficient, although there is a lot of evidence to show that they are efficient enough to render unobtainable on a consistent basis the excess profits that technical analysts claim can be generated from predicting future prices on the basis of past price patterns.

TERM

The length of time until the specific date when a BOND matures; that is, the principal is repaid.

TERM STRUCTURE OF INTEREST RATES

The relationship between the maturity of notes and bonds and the interest rates they offer. Several theories are advanced about this, all of which have some use.

Expectations theory. The interest rate on a long-term BOND will equal the average of rates on a succession of short-term bonds, assuming all the bonds pay the same COUPON. So the interest rate on a three-year bond would be the average of the known rate for a one-year bond plus the implied rates for bonds which become one-year instruments in years two and three. This sounds unnecessarily complex, but the implication is that someone who wants to buy a three-year bond might just as well buy a succession of three one-year bonds, or buy a five-year bond and sell it after three years. The result should be the same. The trouble is that the theory only implies that future rates will come to pass; it does not say that they will. So people who want to invest for, say, three years through buying a succession of three one-year bonds face risks each time they have to switch bonds.

Liquidity preference theory. Lenders prefer to lend for the short term and borrowers prefer to borrow for the long term. So lenders get a premium to be persuaded to lend LONG and borrowers receive a discount for borrowing SHORT. Thus the theory acknowledges RISK in a way that expectations theory does not and explains why the YIELD CURVE should slope upwards.

Market segmentation theory. Particular types of investors focus their activities in particular maturity segments of the market. Banks invest in short-term bonds. Life insurers invest long because they have long-term liabilities they can identify well in advance. Those areas of the market for which there are few natural investors are fairly friendless, so interest rates there are higher. It is a useful theory in so far as it helps explain why the yield curve is often humped around some maturities.

TESSA

See TAX-EXEMPT SPECIAL SAVINGS ACCOUNT.

TEXAS HEDGE

A strategy used in options trading, so-called possibly because it is not a HEDGE at all (but how many real hedges do you see in Texas?). At least, it is not a hedge when employed in isolation. However, when it is combined with the purchase or sale of the underlying STOCK in question it can create ARBITRAGE opportunities. A Texas hedge essentially uses options to give exposure which would be the same as dealing in the actual stock; in other words, "synthetic" stock is created.

For example, a synthetic LONG stock position can be engineered by simultaneously buying call options and selling (that is, underwriting) put options in a stock with the same EXERCISE PRICE and expiry date. Both sides of this transaction bet on the stock price rising. If it does, the profit potential is unlimited, but if the price falls the losses are potentially unlimited, too. Unless, that is, the strategy is combined with the simultaneous SHORT SELLING of the underlying stock. Then the use of the money received up until the purchase of the stock forced by selling the PUT OPTION may create arbitrage profits.

In investing money, the amount of interest you want should depend on whether you want to eat well or sleep well.
J. Kenfield Morley, *Some Things I Believe*

TICK
The smallest price move that a market's regulations will allow in a financial product that the market trades. The term is primarily confined to the currencies and FUTURES markets. On London's futures market, LIFFE, for example, the tick size on the FTSE 100 Index contract is half a point; that is, from 3810.0 to 3810.5 or 3809.5. In the LONG gilts contract it is £0.03 and in interest rate contracts it is one basis point; that is, one-hundredth of a percentage point.

TIME VALUE
One of the core tenets of investment – and, indeed, capitalism – that money has a time value,

meaning that money received in the present is intrinsically more valuable than money received in the future. It is the economic expression of the "Bird in the Hand" proverb and in order to calculate what the "two in the bush" are worth an appropriate DISCOUNT RATE must be used. In other words, if an investor's expected rate of return is 10% per year then clearly that investor would reject the offer of £109 in a year's time instead of £100 today, would be indifferent about receiving £110 in a year or £100 today and would accept £111 one year hence in preference to £100 today.

In options, time value is one of the two components of the price that investors pay to acquire an OPTION to buy or sell a STOCK at a specific price at some point in the future. Time value equals the price of the option (the PREMIUM, to use the jargon) minus the option's INTRINSIC VALUE. If a stock currently trades at 95p and if the market price of the right, but not the obligation, to buy the stock on or before a specific date at 90p is currently 8p, that price comprises 5p of intrinsic value and 3p of time value. The intrinsic value derives from the fact that the price at which the option can be exercised is 5p less than the market price. The time value is the residual amount and is what the buyer pays for the privilege of being able to make profits during the time until the option expires; and that will primarily depend on price movements in the underlying security.

Time value is also known as speculative value.

TOBIN'S Q
Named after a Yale academic, James Tobin, "Q" measures the ratio of the stockmarket value of the debt and equity that a company employs to the replacement cost of the company's tangible assets. Thus a ratio above 1 would attract capital into building assets because those assets would be valued at more than their cost by the market. For a ratio below 1, it would be more profitable to build businesses by acquisition than by capital spending. Tobin's Q has little meaning when applied to individual companies. However, when applied to a

stockmarket as a whole it indicates cheapness or expensiveness. That said, as companies in the developed economies increasingly spend more on RESEARCH AND DEVELOPMENT per dollar of revenue and less on tangible assets, it is debatable whether a ratio of above 1 has as much predictive value as it seemed to do in the 1960s and 1970s.

TOPIX

Shorthand for Tokyo Stock Price Index, the broadest measure of share values on the TOKYO STOCK EXCHANGE. It is an index of all stocks quoted on the "first section" of the Tokyo exchange (that is, about 1,000 larger issues). It measures changes in the market value of Tokyo stocks against a base value struck in 1969, after adjusting for factors such as the conversion of convertible securities. Arguably, therefore, it gives a more accurate measure of the value of the Tokyo exchange than the more widely quoted NIKKEI 225 Index.

TOKYO STOCK EXCHANGE

When Japanese STOCK prices peaked at the end of 1989 Tokyo briefly eclipsed the NEW YORK STOCK EXCHANGE (NYSE) as the world's biggest exchange, as measured by market capitalisation. By the volumes of stocks traded Tokyo is still the biggest, although this is arguably a false measure as the average price of Japanese stocks is much lower than their US counterparts. The Tokyo exchange was the world's third biggest at the end of 1999 with a market capitalisation of $4,325 billion compared with $11,160 billion for the NYSE.

Trading is divided into two "sections", the first of which is for about 1,000 larger issues which are traded at special posts on the floor of the exchange. About 150 of these are traded via an auction system conducted by brokers acting for clients. Sometimes, however, brokers trade for their own account, thus creating a quasi-market making system. Furthermore, the remaining stocks of the first section plus those in the second section (issues for newer and smaller companies) are traded on a computerised execution system.

TOUCH

In the London stockmarket, jargon for the best BID
PRICE and OFFER PRICE for a share quoted by competing market makers. For example, if many firms
make a market in a leading company's shares,
among them might be bids of anything between,
say, 346p and 349p to buy the share and offers of
anything from 351p to 354p to sell it. The touch in
this case would be 349–351p, regardless of which
and how many firms bid or offer the most competitive prices.

TRACKER FUND

UK terminology for INDEX FUND.

TRADED OPTION

See OPTION.

TRADING COLLAR

A means by which a stockmarket protects itself
against potentially destablising trades in its related
OPTIONS or FUTURES markets. For example, on the
NEW YORK STOCK EXCHANGE trading collars are insti-
tuted when on any trading day the DOW JONES IN-
DUSTRIAL AVERAGE moves up or down by at least 2%
from its previous day's close. If the Dow falls by
2%, then the collar requires all INDEX ARBITRAGE
orders to sell stocks that are components of the
S&P 500 INDEX to be at a price not lower than the
previous sell price. If the Dow rises by 2%, then
the collar requires all buy orders to be at a price
higher than the last sell price. Trading collars are
removed if the index returns to within 1% of its
previous day's close. The specific number of
points change in the Dow needed to trigger a
trading collar is set in January, April, June and
October, based in the closing values of the index
for the previous month.

TRANSACTION COSTS

Much investment theory ignores transaction costs,
assuming, as it does, perfect markets where information glides freely and the costs of buying and
selling investments are zero. The trouble is the

real world is not like that. Transaction costs add a significant amount to the cost of dealing and, therefore, affect the net returns available on investments. In well-developed stockmarkets the major transaction cost is often that of bearing the mark-up charged by wholesalers (MARKET MAKERS) who are almost always ready to deal in a STOCK. Behind this come agents' fees for carrying out the business, taxes on these fees and, quite possibly, a charge levied by the stock exchange itself to maintain its own infrastructure.

TREASURY BILL

A short-term debt instrument used by both US and UK central banks to raise money and, more importantly, to regulate interest rates. Treasury bills are discounted securities, meaning they are sold at less than face value and the return to buyers comes from their receiving face value of the bills on maturity. In the UK this is always 91 days after issue but in the United States it may be after three, six or 12 months. Because the chances of either central bank defaulting on its repayment is just about zero, Treasury bills also function as a benchmark for the RISK-FREE RATE OF RETURN.

TREASURY BOND

A fixed-interest security used to meet the US Treasury's long-term funding needs. Treasury bonds have maturities of anything from ten to 30 years. As at March 31st 2000 $653 billion of these bonds were outstanding, representing about 20% of the Treasury's marketable debt. Treasury bonds are issued at par, with institutions bidding for them on a yield basis (the lower the bid, the higher is the yield). Interest on them is paid at six-monthly intervals.

TREASURY NOTE

With maturities on issue of anything between two and ten years, Treasury notes are the US Treasury's intermediate form of debt. Like Treasury bonds they are issued at par; unlike some Treasury bonds, however, they have only one specific maturity date and therefore can be used by some investors to match their assets with their liabilities. As at March 31st 2000 there were $1,733 billion of Treasury notes outstanding, representing about 53% of the Treasury's marketable debt.

A national debt, if it be not excessive, will be a national blessing.

Alexander Hamilton, the first US Treasury Secretary

TULIPMANIA

A famous speculative bubble that took place in the Netherlands in the period 1634–37, during which time the price of best-quality tulip bulbs rose to the equivalent of $16,000 each. Tulips had been introduced into Europe from Turkey in the mid-1500s, but became fashionable among wealthy Dutch society in the early 17th century when diseased bulbs that produced unusually patterned flowers appeared. These could not be reproduced through seeds but only through budding the mother bulb, thus highly unusual bulbs may have had some propagative value. However, by late 1636 speculation spread to even common bulbs and the worst losses were suffered by those who had speculated in these. Prices of best-quality bulbs also fell rapidly, but possibly by no more than would have been expected as bulbs proliferated through propagation.

U

UNIT TRUST

An investment vehicle with two different meanings depending on which side of the Atlantic you are situated.

- In the UK, a unit trust is the generic name for a MUTUAL FUND.
- In the United States, a unit trust – its full name is unit investment trust – is an unmanaged portfolio of assets, usually bonds, often with a fixed life in which units of, say $1,000 a piece, are sold. The assets generally remain unchanged. Although redemption of units is possible, it is more likely that the trust's sponsors will arrange a secondary market in units to avoid liquidating too much of the trust's portfolio.

UNSYSTEMATIC RISK

The investment risks that can be largely eliminated by holding a diversified portfolio of investments; the point being that separate factors will depress different investments at different times, thus changes in their value will not be synchronised. Within stockmarket investment, three factors cover most elements of unsystematic risk.

1 Business risk. Domestic and global economic cycles will influence individual companies differently. A sharp rise in commodity prices will benefit commodity producers, but companies that process commodities will simultaneously suffer if they are caught by higher input prices which they cannot pass on to their customers.

2 Financial risk. Take one company operating with a great deal of debt in its BALANCE SHEET and another which has surplus cash. Other things being equal, their share prices would move in opposite directions if there were a marked rise in interest rates.

3 Liquidity risk. Some investments are easier to buy and sell than others because there is a ready market for them. Those which are difficult to trade (that is, have poor liquidity) are more vulnerable when values fall and therefore risky. In stockmarket terms, government bonds or Treasury bills can almost always be traded and so have little liquidity risk. Conversely, the shares of companies which trade only on OVER-THE-COUNTER markets have a great deal of such risk.

VALUE INVESTING

Caricatured as buying a dollar for 50 cents, or BOTTOM FISHING, value investing is a broad church that defies conventional definitions. It is more about a frame of mind than specific investment techniques, which was best summed up by BENJAMIN GRAHAM when he coined the maxim "Margin of Safety" to encapsulate the value approach. By this he meant that there must be a substantial difference between the price paid for a share by an investor and the investor's assessment of its true value, even though the methods of assessing that value may vary widely. The popular image of value investors – that they seek out the shares of companies whose stockmarket value is less than the BALANCE SHEET value of their shareholders' EQUITY – is only partly true. For example, arguably today's best-known value investor, WARREN BUFFETT, values companies on the fairly conventional assessment of the present value of their future cashflows. But to the extent that he insists on securing the margin of safety between what he is paying and what he is getting he is a value investor.

> *The greatest of all gifts is the power to estimate things at their true worth.*
> La Rochefoucauld,
> *Réflexions; ou sentences et maximes morales*

VALUE LINE COMPOSITE INDEX

A hybrid stockmarket index, which in large part explains the interest in it. This is an index with a base value of 100 as at June 1961 of about 1,700 companies, all of which are quoted on major US exchanges. However, it differs from all other indexes because the major factor affecting its value is the daily percentage changes in the STOCK prices of its constituent companies. There is no weighting for the stockmarket values of its constituents (as with the S&P 500 INDEX), nor is the size of the stock price relevant (as with the DOW JONES INDUSTRIAL AVERAGE). Therefore a 10% change in a stock whose price is $5 and whose stockmarket capitalisation is $500m will have the same effect as a 10% change in a stock with a $10 price and a $1 billion market value. Thus the effect is to measure stockmarket VOLATILITY and, sure enough, the Value Line index is the most volatile of the major indexes. This also makes it an interesting index against which to speculate in the FUTURES market.

VANILLA

The no-frills version of an investment. If it were a BOND then the plain vanilla version would be a standard fixed-income security issued at near par, paying half-yearly dividends and maturing at a specific date when it would be repaid at par (that is, $100 would be repaid for every $100 nominal of STOCK). If it were a CLOSED-END FUND then its capital structure would simply comprise ordinary shares, which would have exclusive rights to both the stream of income from the company's investments and any capital gains.

VARIANCE

A number that defines the extent to which a series of numbers are dispersed around (vary from) their average. It is a key component for measuring RISK in a security or a portfolio, where variance calculates how far an investment's returns for specific periods have varied from its average returns for the whole period under review. Basically, the bigger the number, the more volatile and, therefore, the riskier is the investment. The limitation of variance as a statistical measure is that it is expressed in terms of the square of the series of numbers involved, which is not always easy to grasp. The variance of returns on a portfolio, for example, would be in squares of percentages rather than just percentages. Hence the wider use of STANDARD DEVIATION as a basic measure of risk which, because it is the square root of the variance, measures dispersion in the same values as the average itself.

V

VOLATILITY

The propensity for the market price of an ASSET to bounce around. Volatility is a key factor in many of the arithmetic models that seek to justify current market prices or predict future ones. Since volatility equates to the variability of returns from an investment, it is an acceptable substitute for RISK; the greater the volatility, the greater is the risk that an investment will not turn out as hoped because its market price happens to be on the downswing of a bounce at the time that it needs to be cashed in. The problem is that future volatility is hard to predict and measures of past volatility can, themselves, be variable, depending on how frequently returns are measured (weekly or monthly, for example) and for how long. Therefore, putting expectations of future volatility into predictive models is of limited use, but resorting to using past levels of volatility is equally limited.

Yet two of the best-known and most widely used price models in investment analysis – the BLACK-SCHOLES OPTION PRICING MODEL and the CAPITAL ASSET PRICING MODEL – use a measure of volatility as the sole variable in their equations; the STANDARD DEVIATION in the Black-Scholes model and BETA in the CAP-M. This by no means renders these models useless, but it does mean their results should be treated with caution.

Volatility per se, be it related to weather, portfolio returns, or the timing of one's morning newspaper delivery, is simply a benign statistical probability factor that tells us nothing about risk until coupled with a consequence.
Robert H. Jeffrey

WALL STREET CRASH

There have been many crashes on Wall Street, with 1873, 1907, 1949 and 1987 prominent among them, but there has been only one Wall Street Crash. This epithet describes the period from September to November 1929 when the stockmarket, as measured by the DOW JONES INDUSTRIAL AVERAGE, fell 48% from its peak of 381.2 on September 3rd to 198.7 on November 13th. During these ten weeks there were two days – October 28th and 29th – when the industrial average fell 13.5% and 11.7% respectively. These were the two worst days in the history of the Dow after 1914 until BLACK MONDAY.

The background to the crash was a period of sustained easy money and rising prosperity, which propelled the market up, so that the industrial average doubled in the two years to the start of 1929 and added another 25% before it peaked. The crash then went on to drag the economy into recession, which developed into the Great Depression of the 1930s and which, in turn, pulled the market down further till the industrial average bottomed out in July 1932, having lost 87% of its value from its September 1929 peak.

> *The stockmarket represents everything that anybody has ever hoped, feared or loved, it is all of life.*
>
> Edward C. Johnson II, owner of Fidelity Funds

WARRANT

A warrant, much like a CALL OPTION, gives the holder the right, but not the obligation, to subscribe for ordinary shares almost always, although not necessarily, in the issuing company. The main differences compared with options are that warrants have much longer maturities (typically anything from three to ten years) and are generally issued by a company and therefore raise new money for it. Over the years they have swung in and out of fashion, most recently being much favoured by Japanese companies, which attached warrants to EUROBOND issues during the 1980s BULL market, and by UK investment trusts, which habitually attach them to new share issues. In both cases warrants function as a sweetener to the issue. This meant that in the case of Japanese Eurobonds, the issues could be sold at a lower interest rate than otherwise would have applied. Their function in UK investment trust (CLOSED-END FUND) issues is to close the discount to net asset value at which investment trust shares usually trade in the market.

When used as sweetener, warrants are habitually, although misleadingly, referred to as "free". They seem to create value for shareholders because the warrants themselves have a market value which, when combined with the market value of the new shares, gives an overall increase in value. What is really happening is that the shareholders are being given tomorrow's jam today. Eventually the warrants will be converted into ordinary shares and have a claim on the company's assets, but if conversion is still far into the future that claim will probably not be recognised in the current share price. Hence the illusion of value created.

For anyone who doubts the illusion, consider the effect when the warrants are converted. Imagine that a company has net assets of 100p a share and issues warrants on a one-for-five basis to be converted in five years' time at 120p a share. Assume that during those five years the corporation's net assets grow at 15% a year. At the end of the period net assets would be 200p a share. But converting the warrants into shares at 120p each would have the effect of cutting net assets to 187p a share. Thus the dilution in the future equalises the "value" created upfront.

Nevertheless, warrants have genuine merits as an investment, primarily because they add LEVERAGE to an investment situation. This is a function of the fact that the price of a warrant always trades below the price of a share into which it converts, yet its price is inextricably linked to that share. As an example, take a company with shares which

trade at 90p and warrants which trade at 20p.
Assume also that the conversion price is 120p.
Under these circumstances no one would convert
their warrants. But if the share price doubled to
180p then the warrants would have INTRINSIC VALUE
and conversion would be a sensible proposition.
Now the warrants must trade at 60p minimum
(share price less conversion price). For them to do
less would mean that an opportunity for ARBITRAGE
would be created. An investor could sell the
shares, buy the warrants, convert and pocket the
difference. However, in this scenario, although
the share price has doubled, the warrant price has
tripled. As always with leverage, the downside is
magnified as well. So if the share price halved to
45p the warrant price would fall much further.
How much further would depend largely on how
long there was to the warrants' expiry. For a short-
dated warrant on a share with pretty glum
prospects, the value would probably be little more
than nominal.

WEIGHT OF MONEY
A backstop explanation of why a stockmarket is
moving upwards. If all else fails the "weight of
money" argument is always worth a try because
no one can disprove it and it has plausibility. Just
as growth in an economy's money supply may
well lead to higher prices for goods and services,
it is reasonable to assume that extra money in the
hands of big investors will lead to higher prices
for stocks. Thus cashflows into and out of savings
institutions are monitored by investment analysts
as a factor that may influence prices.

WEIGHTED AVERAGE COST OF CAPITAL
If a company is to succeed, in the long run its
profits must exceed its cost of capital. Working
out this cost means using the CAPITAL ASSET PRICING
MODEL to calculate a DISCOUNT RATE for the cost of
its EQUITY and taking the actual average interest
rate on its debt. These two charges are then
weighted according to the proportion of equity
and debt in the total capital.

WILSHIRE 5000 INDEX

The most broadly based of all US COMMON STOCK price indexes. Despite its name, it includes over 7,000 stocks, basically all those quoted on the NEW YORK STOCK EXCHANGE, with the balance made up from stocks on NASDAQ and some OVER-THE-COUNTER stocks. It is weighted for the market value of its constituents and currently includes stocks with an aggregate market value of $14.1 trillion as at October 1999. In comparison, the value of companies contained in the S&P 500 INDEX was $11.3 trillion.

WRITER

The person who issues (writes) an options contract and who assumes most of the RISK in much the same way as an insurance company in normal casualty business. Writers come in two forms.

- Covered, meaning that because of their own arrangements their risk, like that of the purchaser of the options contract, is limited.
- Naked, meaning that their potential liability is unlimited if things do not go the way they planned.

Someone who writes a CALL OPTION agrees to sell an amount of STOCK at a particular price within a specified period. In return he gets a fee upfront. He is betting that the price of the stock concerned will not rise much during the period in question. If he is right and he is covered (meaning here that he owns the stock in question) then he will effectively improve his return on the stock. If he is wrong and the stock is "called away" from him, he will forgo extra profits as the stock's price continues to rise. Should he face an uncovered, or naked, call then his losses will be the difference between the market price of the stock to him less the PREMIUM he has received and the value of the contract's EXERCISE PRICE.

Writing a PUT OPTION means that the writer agrees to buy stock within the terms of the contract. He is betting that the stock's price will rise.

If he is wrong then he will have to buy stock at above the market price and will face losses unless he has covered his position by SHORT SELLING the stock.

YIELD CURVE

The graphical representation of the yield on bonds of increasing maturities. On the chart time runs from left to right and yield is shown on the vertical axis. Thus, at a glance, investors can get an impression of the maturities where demand is strong and vice versa. Yield curves, which are used mainly for analysis of government bonds, are put together by REGRESSION ANALYSIS of the various yields and maturities available. This is flawed to the extent that more information may be available for some maturities than for others. However, the overall picture can indicate which way investors expect interest rates to move.

Classically, the curve should slope upward as investors demand an increasing reward the longer they lend. A downward-sloping curve indicates that shorter-term interest rates are high and expected to fall. In practical terms, especially in the UK, the yield curve is "humped" in the range of seven- to ten-year maturities. This fits with the idea that short-dated government bonds are sought by banks for liquidity and regulatory requirements, whereas long-dated bonds are bought by pensions funds with liabilities stretching far into the future. In comparison, demand for medium-dated bonds is modest, hence the higher yields which the market demands to buy these securities. (See TERM STRUCTURE OF INTEREST RATES.)

YIELD GAP

A measure of the cheapness or expensiveness of equities versus government bonds, expressed as the YIELD TO MATURITY on government bonds minus the DIVIDEND YIELD on ordinary shares. Other factors aside, the narrower the gap between the two, the cheaper the equities would be. For example, just before the stockmarket crash of October 1987, when (with the benefit of hindsight) equities were expensive, the yield gap in the United States was over seven percentage points. After share prices collapsed, and implicitly became cheap again, the gap narrowed to about four points.

It is nowadays the norm for bonds to yield more than equities. However, in the low-inflation 1950s when this benchmark started to be measured the opposite was often the case; risky shares yielded more than "safe" bonds. Thus the yield gap started life as share yields minus bond yields, so on rare occasions when bonds yielded more than equities the sum produced a minus figure which was known as the "reverse yield gap". With the passage of time, the acceleration of inflation and a consistently higher yield on bonds, the sum was turned on its head and the expression "reverse yield gap" all but forgotten.

YIELD SPREAD

The difference in yield between bonds of similar COUPON and TERM. Mostly this is owing to investors' qualitative assessment of respective borrowers: the Bundesbank will almost always be able to borrow more cheaply than the Bank of England; the US Treasury will borrow more cheaply than a top-quality corporation. Other factors also play a part: bonds with poor marketability will trade at higher yields than particularly liquid issues; if a government funds its debt heavily in a particular maturity range this will narrow the spread between itself and corporate borrowers.

YIELD TO MATURITY

Technically, the DISCOUNT RATE at which all outlays and receipts on a redeemable security net out at a present value of zero. Thus yield to maturity takes account of regular payments of income and capital gain or loss on redemption. Hence the term redemption yield in the UK. It is also the INTERNAL RATE OF RETURN. Take a BOND with five years to redemption standing at $123 in the market and paying semi-annual dividends of $6.50 for every $100 of nominal stock held (that is, $13 a year). Its running yield would be 10.6% ($13 as a percentage of $123). However, assuming the bond was repaid at $100, its yield to maturity would be only 7.4% to take account of the fact that the $23 of capital loss has to be written off over its remaining life.

ZERO-COUPON BOND

An innovation of the early 1980s which can be useful for financial planning because it offers a lump-sum payment at a specified date in the future. Thus, for example, a company might issue zero-coupon bonds at $60 each with the promise that in seven years it will repay $100 for every $60 borrowed. Such a BOND would have a YIELD TO MATURITY of virtually 7.5% per year; that is the compound rate at which value would accrue to the bond for it to reach $100 in seven years' time. Zeros have the added feature that they are particularly sensitive to changes in interest rates during their life, therefore they can be a good speculation for anyone betting on interest rates falling. However, in the United States the value that accrues to the bond each year is subject to tax, unless the bond is sheltered in a tax-free account.

In the UK, where zeros are most often issued as zero-dividend preference shares by investment trusts, big investors get the same tax treatment as in the United States. For small-scale investors, though, the gains that accrue are still taxed as a capital gain on maturity, which is generally preferable to taxing them annually against income.

1 Stockmarket returns

UK

	Average growth (% per year)	Standard deviation (%)	Compound growth (% per year)	Down years
1918–25	12	24	9	2
1926–35	6	18	4	4
1936–45	2	12	1	4
1946–55	6	15	5	4
1956–65	7	21	5	6
1966–75	14	51	4	5
1976–85	17	15	16	1
1986–95	11	12	10	2
Total period	**9**	**25**	**7**	**28**

United States

	Average growth (% per year)	Standard deviation (%)	Compound growth (% per year)	Down years
1915–25	7	21	5	5
1926–35	6	36	–1	4
1936–45	5	19	3	4
1946–55	11	14	10	3
1956–65	8	15	7	3
1966–75	1	19	–1	4
1976–85	7	14	6	4
1986–95	13	12	13	1
Total period	**7**	**20**	**5**	**27**

Source: UK index: BZW Equity index; US index: Dow Jones Industrial Average.

2 Stockmarket performances

UK[a]

Year end	FTSE A All-Share	Change (% per year)	FTSE 100 Index[b]	Change (% per year)
1970	136.3	−7.5		
1971	193.4	41.9		
1972	218.2	12.8		
1973	149.8	−31.4		
1974	66.9	−55.3		
1975	158.1	136.3		
1976	152.0	−3.9		
1977	214.5	41.2		
1978	220.2	2.7	484.2	
1979	229.8	4.3	509.2	5.2
1980	292.0	27.1	647.4	27.1
1981	313.1	7.2	684.3	5.7
1982	382.2	22.1	834.3	21.9
1983	470.5	23.1	1,000	19.9
1984	592.9	26.0	1,232.2	23.2
1985	682.9	15.2	1,412.6	14.6
1986	835.5	22.3	1,679	18.9
1987	870.2	4.2	1,712.7	2.0
1988	926.6	6.5	1,793.1	4.7
1989	1,204.7	30.0	2,422.7	35.1
1990	1,032.3	−14.3	2,143.5	−11.5
1991	1,187.7	15.1	2,493.1	16.3
1992	1,363.8	14.8	2,846.5	14.2
1993	1,682.2	23.3	3,418.4	20.1
1994	1,521.4	−9.6	3,065.5	−10.3
1995	1,803.1	18.5	3,689.3	20.3
1996	2,013.7	11.7	4,118.5	11.6
1997	2,411.0	19.7	5,135.5	24.7
1998	2,673.9	10.9	5,882.6	14.5
1999	3,242.1	21.2	6,930.2	17.8
Compound growth (% per year)		11.6		13.5
Average change (% per year)		15.3		14.1
Standard deviation (% per year)		30.7		11.5

a Changes in capital value only.
b "FTSE" is a registered trademark of the London Stock Exchange Ltd and the Financial Times Ltd and is used by FTSE International Ltd under licence.

United States[a]

Year end	S&P 500 Index[b]	Change (% per year)	Dow Jones Industrial Average	Change (% per year)	NASDAQ 100	Change (% per year)
1970	92.2	0.1	838.9	4.8		
1971	102.1	10.8	890.2	6.1		
1972	118.1	15.6	1,020.0	14.6		
1973	97.6	−17.4	848.0	−16.9		
1974	68.6	−29.7	616.2	−27.3		
1975	90.2	31.5	852.4	38.3		
1976	107.5	19.1	1,004.7	17.9		
1977	95.1	−11.5	831.2	−17.3		
1978	96.1	1.1	805.0	−3.1		
1979	107.9	12.3	838.7	4.2		
1980	135.8	25.8	964.0	14.9		
1981	122.6	−9.7	875.0	−9.2		
1982	140.6	14.8	1,046.6	19.6		
1983	164.9	17.3	1,258.6	20.3	133.1	
1984	167.2	1.4	1,211.6	−3.7	108.6	−18.4
1985	211.3	26.3	1,546.7	27.7	132.3	21.8
1986	242.2	14.6	1,896.0	22.6	141.4	6.9
1987	247.1	2.0	1,938.8	2.3	156.3	10.5
1988	277.7	12.4	2,168.6	11.8	177.4	13.5
1989	353.4	27.3	2,753.2	27.0	223.8	26.2
1990	330.2	−6.6	2,633.7	−4.3	199.4	−10.9
1991	417.1	26.3	3,168.8	20.3	326.7	63.8
1992	435.7	4.5	3,301.1	4.2	360.2	10.3
1993	466.5	7.1	3,754.1	13.7	398.3	10.6
1994	459.3	−1.5	3,834.4	2.1	404.3	1.5
1995	615.9	34.1	5,117.1	33.5	576.2	42.5
1996	740.7	20.3	6,448.3	26.0	821.4	42.6
1997	970.4	31.0	7,908.3	22.6	990.8	20.6
1998	1,229.2	26.7	9,181.4	16.1	1,836.0	85.3
1999	1,469.3	19.5	11,497.1	25.2	3,707.8	101.9
Compound growth (% per year)		10.0		9.5		23.1
Average change (% per year)		11.2		10.7		26.8
Standard deviation (% per year)		15.9		16.0		33.1

a Changes in capital value only.
b S&P 500 is a registered trademark of the McGraw-Hill Companies, Inc.

	Japan[a]			Hong Kong[ab]	
Year end	Nikkei 225 Average	Change (% per year)		Hang Seng Index	Change (% per year)
1970	1,987.1	−15.8		211.6	36.5
1971	2,713.7	36.6		336.9	59.2
1972	5,207.9	91.9		843.4	150.4
1973	4,306.8	−17.3		433.7	−48.6
1974	3,817.2	−11.4		171.1	−60.5
1975	4,358.6	14.2		350.0	104.5
1976	4,987.5	14.4		447.7	27.9
1977	4,865.6	−2.4		404.0	−9.8
1978	6,001.9	23.4		495.5	22.6
1979	6,569.7	9.5		879.4	77.5
1980	7,063.1	7.5		1,473.6	67.6
1981	7,681.8	8.8		1,405.8	−4.6
1982	8,016.7	4.4		783.8	−44.2
1983	9,893.8	23.4		874.9	11.6
1984	11,542.6	16.7		1,200.4	37.2
1985	13,083.2	13.3		1,752.5	46.0
1986	18,820.6	43.9		2,568.3	46.6
1987	21,564.0	14.6		2,302.8	−10.3
1988	30,159.0	39.9		2,687.4	16.7
1989	38,915.9	29.0		2,836.6	5.5
1990	23,848.7	−38.7		3,024.6	6.6
1991	22,983.8	−3.6		4,297.3	42.1
1992	16,925.0	−26.4		5,512.4	28.3
1993	17,417.2	2.9		11,888.4	115.7
1994	19,723.1	13.2		8,191.0	−31.1
1995	19,868.2	0.7		10,073.4	23.0
1996	19,361.0	−2.6		13,451.0	33.5
1997	15,259.0	−21.2		10,723.0	−20.3
1998	13,842.2	−9.3		10,048.6	−6.3
1999	18,934.3	36.8		16,692.1	66.1
Compound growth (% per year)		8.1			16.3
Average change (% per year)		10.8			26.0
Standard deviation (% per year)		25.3			49.0

a Changes in capital value only.
b HSI Services Ltd.

Canada[a]			Germany[b]	
Year end	Toronto Composite Index	Change (% per year)	DAX Index	Change (% per year)
1970	985.8	–6.4	443.9	–28.7
1971	1,026.5	4.1	473.5	6.7
1972	1,252.2	22.0	536.4	13.3
1973	1,207.5	–3.6	396.3	–26.1
1974	885.9	–26.6	401.8	1.4
1975	973.8	9.9	563.3	40.2
1976	1,012.1	3.9	509.0	–9.6
1977	1,059.6	4.7	549.3	7.9
1978	1,310.0	23.6	575.2	4.7
1979	1,813.2	38.4	497.8	–13.5
1980	2,268.7	25.1	480.9	–3.4
1981	1,954.2	–13.9	490.4	2.0
1982	1,985.0	1.6	552.8	12.7
1983	2,552.3	28.6	774.0	40.0
1984	2,400.3	–6.0	820.9	6.1
1985	2,900.6	20.8	1,366.2	66.4
1986	3,066.1	5.7	1,432.3	4.8
1987	3,160.1	3.1	1,000.0	–30.2
1988	3,390.0	7.3	1,327.9	32.8
1989	3,969.8	17.1	1,790.4	34.8
1990	3,256.8	–18.0	1,398.2	–21.9
1991	3,512.4	7.8	1,578.0	12.9
1992	3,350.4	–4.6	1,545.1	–2.1
1993	4,321.4	29.0	2,266.7	46.7
1994	4,213.6	–2.5	2,106.6	–7.1
1995	4,713.5	11.9	2,253.9	7.0
1996	5,927.0	25.7	2,888.7	28.2
1997	6,699.4	13.0	4,249.7	47.1
1998	6,485.9	–3.2	5,002.3	17.7
1999	8,413.8	29.7	6,958.1	39.1
Compound growth (% per year)		7.7		10.0
Average change (% per year)		8.8		12.4
Standard deviation (% per year)		15.6		23.7

a Changes in capital value only.
b Total return index.

Emerging markets[a]   France[ab]

Year end	IFC Composite	Change (% per year)	CAC 40 Index	Change (% per year)
1987			1,000.0	
1988	231.0		1,579.9	58.0
1989	353.4	53.0	2,001.1	26.7
1990	240.6	−31.9	1,517.9	−24.1
1991	277.4	15.3	1,765.7	16.3
1992	280.9	1.3	1,857.8	5.2
1993	459.0	63.4	2,268.2	22.1
1994	448.0	−2.4	1,881.2	−17.1
1995	370.4	−17.3	1,872.0	−0.5
1996	388.9	5.0	2,315.7	23.7
1997	321.4	−17.4	2,998.9	29.5
1998	252.9	−21.3	3,942.7	31.5
1999	402.3	59.1	5,958.3	51.1
Compound growth (% per year)		5.2		16.0
Average change (% per year)		9.7		14.9
Standard deviation (% per year)		34.1		22.2

The world

Year end	FTSE W World	Change (% per year)	Year end	FTSE W World	Change (% per year)
1986	100.0		**1993**	149.9	17.7
1987	99.1	−0.9	**1994**	146.7	−2.1
1988	123.2	24.3	**1995**	170.1	16.0
1989	151.3	22.8	**1996**	194.2	14.2
1990	115.6	−23.6	**1997**	231.6	19.3
1991	132.3	14.4	**1998**	272.7	17.7
1992	127.4	−3.7	**1999**	344.7	26.4

Compound growth (% per year)		11.3
Average change (% per year)		13.0
Standard deviation (% per year)		20.4

a Changes in capital value only.   b SBF, Paris Bourse.

3 Government bond returns and inflation

Total returns; % per year

UK

Year end	Bonds	Inflation	Real return
1981	4.57	11.88	−7.31
1982	41.72	8.60	33.12
1983	13.61	4.61	9.00
1984	8.87	4.97	3.90
1985	12.01	6.08	5.93
1986	11.53	3.41	8.12
1987	15.27	4.14	11.13
1988	6.77	4.91	1.86
1989	8.22	7.80	0.42
1990	9.61	9.47	0.14
1991	16.17	5.86	10.31
1992	18.66	3.73	14.93
1993	21.01	1.57	19.44
1994	−6.27	2.47	−3.80
1995	16.43	3.41	13.02
1996	7.30	2.45	4.85
1997	14.14	3.13	11.01
1998	19.79	3.42	16.37
1999	−0.92	1.56	−2.48

United States

Year end	Bonds	Inflation	Real return
1981	3.86	10.32	−6.46
1982	31.33	6.16	25.17
1983	4.06	3.21	0.85
1984	14.29	4.32	9.97
1985	28.48	3.56	24.91
1986	21.03	1.86	19.17
1987	−1.37	3.65	−5.02
1988	8.15	4.14	4.01
1989	17.39	4.82	12.57
1990	7.47	5.40	2.07
1991	17.97	4.21	13.76
1992	7.78	3.01	4.77
1993	15.03	2.99	12.04
1994	−2.90	2.56	−0.34
1995	17.42	2.83	14.59
1996	2.91	2.93	−0.02
1997	10.00	2.34	7.66
1998	10.25	1.62	8.63
1999	−2.91	2.20	−5.11

4 The world's leading equity markets, end-1999

Stock exchange	Value ($ billion)	Trading volume ($ billion)	Market index	Closing level	Market P/E ratio	Market yield (%)
Australia						
Australian	428	198	ASX Index	3,153	26.8	3.2
Belgium						
Brussels	184	280	All Share	8,794	18.3	1.7
Canada						
Toronto	789	357	TSE 300	8,414	40.0	1.3
France						
Paris	1,503	709	CAC 40	2,283	24.6	1.8
Germany						
Deutsche	1,432	1,551	DAX Index	6,958	26.0	1.3
Hong Kong	609	230	Hang Seng	16,962	27.9	1.9
Italy						
Milan	728	539	Milan BCI	1,817	29.3	1.5
Japan						
Tokyo	4,455	1,676	Nikkei 225	18,934	83.1	0.6

Mexico						
Mexican	154	35	IPC Mexico	7,130	11.2	1.0
Netherlands						
Amsterdam	695	471	CBS All-Share	933	31.8	1.7
Singapore	198	107	Straits Times	2,480	32.8	1.9
South Africa						
Johannesburg	193	87	JSE Industrials	9,212	17.7	1.8
South Korea	306	733	KOPSI	1,028	...	0.5
Spain						
Madrid	431	739	MSE Price Index	1,009	24.1	1.7
Sweden						
Stockholm	373	314	Veckan All-Share	6,866	25.5	1.3
Switzerland	693	562	SPI	5,023	21.0	1.2
Taiwan	377	914	TSE Index	8,449	33.1	1.0
UK						
London	2,855	3,399	FTSE A All-Share	3,242	28.6	2.1
US						
American	142	276	Amex Composite	877.0	...	...
NASDAQ	5,205	10,467	NASDAQ Composite	4,069	...	...
New York	11,438	8,945	NYSE Composite	650	30.8	1.1

5 Investment formulas

Capital fulcrum point

$$CFP = [(e/s - w)^{1/y} - 1] \times 100\%$$

Where:
e = exercise price
s = share price
w = warrant price
y = years to expiry of warrant

Black-Scholes model

Basic model for calculating the fair value of a call option on a non-dividend paying stock

$$\text{Call price} = S\ [N(d_1)] - E/e^{rt}[N(d_2)]$$

Where:
S = current stock price
$N(d_1)$ = normal distribution function of d_1
E = exercise price of option
e = the base of natural logarithms (= 2.718)
r = risk-free interest at an annual rate
t = time to expiry of option (as a fraction of a year)
$N(d_2)$ = normal distribution function of d_2

To solve for d_1:
$$d_1 = [\ln(S/E) + (r + 0.5sd^2)t]\ /\ [sd(t)^{1/2}]$$
Where:
$\ln(S/E)$ = the natural log of S/E
sd = the standard deviation of annual returns on the share price (where the share price is squared, it is the variance)

To solve for d_2:
$$d_2 = d1 - [sd(t)^{1/2}]$$

Single index model

Shows a security's return as a function of the market's

$$R_{st} = a_s + b_s(R_{mt}) + e_{st}$$

Where:

R_{st} = the return on security $_s$ over period $_t$
a_s = the constant return on security $_s$
b_s = the sensitivity of the security's return to the market's return (ie, its beta)
R_{mt} = the market's return over period $_t$
e_{st} = the difference between the actual return on $_s$ during a given period and its expected return

Capital asset pricing model

$$E(R_s) = RF + \beta_s[E(R_m) - RF]$$

Where:
$E(R_s)$ = the expected return on security $_s$
RF = the risk-free rate of return
β_s = the beta of security $_s$
$E(R_m)$ = the expected return on the market

Capital market line

Shows the expected return from efficient portfolios

$$[E(R_m) - RF]/[sd(R_m)]$$

defines the slope of the market line, where:
$E(R_m)$ = the expected return from the market
RF = the risk-free rate of return
$sd(R_m)$ = the standard deviation of returns from the market

Thus the expected return from any portfolio on the capital market line is:

$$E(R_p) = RF + \{[E(R_m) - RF]/[sd(R_m)]\}sd(R_p)$$

Where:
$E(R_p)$ = the expected return on portfolio $_p$
$sd(R_p)$ = the standard deviation of returns on portfolio $_p$

Dividend discount model

Where the growth rate in dividends is assumed to be constant, the fair price of a common stock can be stated as follows:
$$P = D/(k - g)$$

Where:
P = the price of the stock
D = expected dividend
k = the required rate of return
g = the expected growth rate in dividends

From this, the required rate of return can stated as:
k = (D/P) + g

and the stock's price/earnings ratio as:

P/E = (D/E) / (k − g)

Where:
E = the expected level of earnings

6 Accounting terminology differences

UK	United States
Acquisition accounting	Purchase accounting
Articles of Association	Bylaws
Balance sheet	Statement of financial position
Bills	Notes
Bonus or scrip issue	Stock dividend or stock split
Closing rate method	Current rate method
Creditors	Payables
Debtors	Receivables
Deferred tax	Deferred income tax
Depreciation	Amortisation
Exceptional items	Unusual items
Finance leases	Capital leases
Land and buildings	Real estate
Merger accounting	Pooling of interests
Nominal value	Par value
Non-pension post-employment benefits	OPEBs
Ordinary shares	Common stock
Own shares purchased but not cancelled	Treasury stock
Preference shares	Preferred stock
Profit and loss account	Income statement
Profit for the financial year	Net income
Provisions	Allowances
Share premium	Additional paid-in capital
Shareholders' funds	Stockholders' equity
Stocks	Inventories
Turnover	Revenues
Undistributable reserves	Restricted surplus

Source: UK/US GAAP Comparison (3rd edn), Ernst & Young/Kogan Page.

7 Recommended reading

Highly recommended

Brett, Michael, *How to Read the Financial Pages*, Century Business, 1987

Graham, Benjamin, *The Intelligent Investor* (4th edn), Harper & Row, 1973

Jones, Charles P., *Investments Analysis and Management* (6th edn), John Wiley & Sons, 1985

Malkiel, Burton G., *A Random Walk down Wall Street* (6th edn), W.W. Norton, 1973

"Adam Smith", *The Money Game*, Michael Joseph, 1968

Train, John, *The Money Masters*, Harper & Row, 1980

Others

Cottle, Sidney, Murray, Roger F. and Block, Frank E., *Graham and Dodd's Security Analysis* (5th edn), McGraw-Hill, 1934

Dreman, David, *Contrarian Investment Strategies*, Simon & Schuster, 1998

Ellis, Charles D., *The Investor's Anthology*, John Wiley & Sons, 1997

Elton, Edwin J. and Gruber, Martin J., *Modern Portfolio Theory and Investment Analysis* (4th edn), John Wiley & Sons, 1981

Galbraith, J.K., *The Great Crash*, Penguin Books, 1954

The GT Guide to World Equity Markets, Euromoney Publications, 1994

Hills, Richard, *Hedge Funds*, Rushmere Wynne, 1996

Holmes, Geoffrey and Sugden, Alan, *Interpreting Company Reports and Accounts* (4th edn), Woodhead-Faulkener, 1979

Kolb, Robert W., *Understanding Options*, John Wiley & Sons, 1995

Lefevre, Edwin, *Reminiscences of a Stock Operator*, John Wiley & Sons, 1993

Lofthouse, Stephen, *Equity Investment Management*, John Wiley & Sons, 1994

McHattie, Andrew, *The Investor's Guide to Warrants*, Pitman Publishing, 1992

Pereira, Vivian, Paterson, Ron and Wilson, Allister, *UK/US GAAP Comparison* (3rd edn), Kogan Page, 1990

Rutterford, Janette, *Introduction to Stock Exchange Investment* (2nd edn), The MacMillan Press, 1983

Smith, Terry, *Accounting for Growth*, Century Business, 1992

Stewart, G. Bennett, *The Quest for Value*, Harper Business, 1991

Teweles, Richard J., Bradley, Edward S. and Teweles, Ted M., *The Stockmarket* (6th edn), John Wiley & Sons, 1992

Train, John, *The New Money Masters*, Harper & Row, 1989